THE TOP UK AIR FRYER COOKBOOK FOR BEGINNERS

150 Delicious & Affordable Recipes with European Measurements &
UK Ingredients Including Tips & Tricks for Using Your Air Fryer
Is the part about European measurements & UK ingredients
necessary?

CONTENT

01   Introduction

02   What Is an Air Fryer?

03   What Are the Different Types of Air Fryers?

04   How Do Air Fryers Work?

05   What Can You Cook in Your Air Fryer?

06   How to Use an Air Fryer?

07   What Are the Benefits of Air Fryers?

08   Cooking with Air Fryers: Frequently Asked Questions

09   SECTION 1: VEGAN RECIPES

10   SECTION 2: BREAKFAST

11   SECTION 3: LUNCH RECIPES

12   SECTION 4: DINNER RECIPES

13   SECTION 5: SNACKS

14   Conclusion

ABOUT THE AUTHOR

A group of Chefs trying to make cooking fun and healthy again!

We know how busy you are, that is why we aim to make our recipes as easy, budget friendly and delicious as possible, so you can cook up meals you look forward to that nourish you simultaneously.

With every book we create we also include a Bonus PDF so you get access to coloured images with every single recipe! We couldn't include them in the book due to printing costs and we wanted to keep the books as affordable as possible. We hope you enjoy!

Please email us & our customer support team will help as soon as we possibly can! We want to make sure you are 100% satisfied and if you have any issues at all please email us and we will do our best to help.

Also, if you have any feedback on how we can improve this book & further books please email us that and we will make all the changes we can. As mentioned we can't add colour photos inside the book due to printing costs, but any other improvements we would love to make!

Our customer support email is vicandersonpublishing@gmail.com – as mentioned email us anything you wish here ☺

Happy Cooking!

INTRODUCTION

Healthy cooking can be a challenge. It sometimes feels like we must choose between cooking delicious and cooking healthy.

But then came the air fryers!

Air fryers have squashed this belief that a dish cannot be both tasty and healthy. Air fryers have shown us a way to cook healthy dishes that also taste delicious.

If you are new to an air fryer or are planning to buy one, you may be wondering how to use it and which dishes you can prepare with it. You may have many questions like how to use an air fryer, how to clean it, how to preheat it, and so on. And of course, you also want to get hold of a long list of dishes you can prepare using it.

In this book, you will find 150 recipes you can prepare using your air fryer. I will share recipes you can try for breakfast, lunch, dinner, and also mid-meal snacks. We will cover a wide range of recipes, including meat recipes, seafood recipes, and even vegan recipes so that your platter is always filled with a variety of dishes.

The purpose is to ensure your body gets all the nutrients from different sources so that you can satisfy your taste buds while also taking good care of your health.

In this book, you will also learn how to use your air fryer in the best way. I will also share some tips and tricks so that using an air fryer becomes easy for you.

WHAT IS AN AIR FRYER?

An air fryer is a versatile kitchen appliance you can use to air fry, broil, roast, bake, crisp, reheat, or dehydrate foods. These are basically small, but powerful ovens.

Air fryers are designed based on the concept of cooking using hot air. Just like most other ovens, air fryers also use air as to create heat to cook food. This is in contrast to deep frying, which uses fat or oil as a means to create heat for cooking food.

What makes air fryers special is they can help you eliminate a common concern, which is how to avoid adding too much oil to dishes. We all know that eating high-fat or deep-fried foods can be harmful to our health!

Over the last few years, air fryers have gained a prominent place in many households. An increasing number of families are choosing to cook meals using air fryers. And the reasons are not limited to their desire to eat healthily. Air fryers come with several other benefits. Air fryers are significantly less messy than deep-frying. They can save you time in cooking and cleaning. These little ovens can do much more than simply crank out your faux-fried food. They bring in crackly-skinned chicken wings, beautifully browned vegetables, and even light airy cakes!

And now, with this recipe book, you will be able to do much more using your air fryer, putting it to its best use so that you can keep yourself and your family healthier and happier by serving them healthier and tastier dishes.

WHAT ARE THE DIFFERENT TYPES OF AIR FRYERS?

There are two main types of air fryers: air fryer ovens and basket air fryers.

Air fryer ovens are similar to toaster ovens. They have racks to place food on. Air fryer ovens come with more cooking functions and have more room inside for food. However, being larger in size, they also tend to take up more space in your kitchen.

Basket air fryers have a basket to put food in. The basket is removable, making it easier for you to clean up after cooking.

HOW DO AIR FRYERS WORK?

An air fryer has a built-in heating element, which radiates the heat needed to cook food. It also has a fan that circulates hot air around the food inside the basket or on the top of the rack. The circulation of hot air helps the food cook uniformly. This is quite unlike what happens in the regular ovens in which the heat only tends to rise. This causes the top rack to become the hottest spot, leading to uneven doneness.

The hot air circulation also allows you to cook using significantly less oil than traditional methods of cooking, like deep frying. It ensures the food browns nicely, giving your dishes delicious flavours, especially along the caramelized edges. Above all, it can get you those crunchy and crispy bites you love so much.

WHAT CAN YOU COOK IN YOUR AIR FRYER?

You can cook just about anything in your air fryer! You can use it to prepare protein-rich dishes with chicken, fish, and pork. You can also use it to cook vegetable side dishes, baked goods, and desserts.

The air fryer is specifically suited for preparing dishes that should be extra crispy or crunchy, like French fries, baked potatoes with crispy skins, and fried chicken. It is also a good way to cook meats like steak and chicken, as they turn out to be more flavourful and juicer when cooked in an air fryer.

HOW TO USE AN AIR FRYER?

Most people find it much easier to cook when they have an air fryer. As with any new appliance, you may experience some difficulty initially. But once you get the hang of it, it will surely open up a plethora of recipes that will make cooking more exciting and enjoyable for you.

Here are some tips and tricks you need to keep in mind for using your air fryer correctly:

Avoid overcrowding the basket.

Avoid placing food in the fryer in a stacked or layered manner. Instead, place it in a single layer in the basket or on the shelves. This will promote even cooking and ensure the food is crispy. You can always cook in two or more batches as needed.

Set the fryer at the right temperature.

The general rule of thumb for setting the temperature of your air fryer is to lower it by 25 degrees from the temperature that you normally use while cooking in an oven. You can also follow the instructions mentioned in the manual of your air fryer about the recommended temperatures for different foods.

Dry the foods.

Moisture can affect the crispiness of your dishes. Dry the food well before placing them into the air fryer so that they get perfectly crispy. You can also pat the food dry with paper towels or a clean kitchen towel before adding seasonings or oil and placing it in the fryer.

Preheat your fryer.

Preheating can ensure the food is cooked more evenly. If your air fryer has a preheating option, make sure you preheat it before placing food inside it. This will also reduce the total cooking time.

Choose the right pre-sets.

Most air fryers come with a number of pre-set programs that have cooking temperatures and times for common dishes. You can definitely try these pre-sets and see how it works, or choose your own cooking time and temperature.

Check the food occasionally.

When you are new to using an air fryer, you might want to check whether the food is properly cooked or not a bit more often. Don't hesitate to pull the basket out so that you can check on the progress during the cooking cycle. This is also important to ensure your food is not overcooked.

Shake the basket occasionally.

When you are cooking small pieces of food, like French fries or Brussels sprouts, give the basket a little nudge or a shake about halfway through the cooking time to promote even browning and cooking. When you are cooking larger prices of food, like chicken and pork chops, flip the pieces over once or twice during the cooking period.

IMPORTANT TIPS TO FOLLOW WHEN USING AN AIR FRYER

Avoid greasing the drawer with cooking spray

Most people prefer to grease the drawer with cooking spray. If you want to increase the lifespan of your air fryer, it is best to avoid doing so because the baskets usually have a non-stick coating, which, over time, can get damaged due to the cooking spray. Instead, you can toss your food in a bit of oil. And if you are using an air fryer to cook pre-fried frozen foods, you don't even need the help of extra oil or grease.

Don't overcrowd the shelf

It can be tempting to add another handful of shaved beets and potato sticks to the air fryer shelf. It's best to avoid this temptation and instead, cook in smaller batches so that your dishes come out crisper.

Go slow

Once your food is cooked, avoid any haste in transferring the hot contents from the basket to a bowl. Make sure you use a spoon or tongs to take out the cooked food. If you happen to yank out the basket and empty it onto a platter, the excess oil collected beneath the removable grate in the basket can come spilling out with it and burn your fingers. It can also make a mess while leaving the food greasy.

WHAT ARE THE BENEFITS OF AIR FRYERS?

HEALTHIER COOKING

The most important benefit of using an air fryer is it offers a great way to support healthy cooking. With very little oil used for cooking, air fryers can be the perfect way to replace high-fat, deep-fried foods that are known to raise cholesterol levels. [1] [2]

Research has shown that cooking methods that use less oil, such as air fryers, can help lower your cholesterol levels. This can improve your heart function and control your blood pressure, thus protecting you against life-threatening complications like heart attacks and stroke.

PROMOTE WEIGHT LOSS

Several studies have revealed a strong link between a higher intake of deep-fried foods and the risk of obesity. Fried foods tend to be very high in unhealthy fats, like saturated fats and trans fats. They also have the higher calorie content. Replacing deep-fried foods with air-fried foods can reduce your intake of unhealthy fats and thus, promote weight loss. [3]

REDUCE TOXIC EXPOSURE

Not many people know that cooking in air fryers can reduce the risk of exposure to acrylamide. When you cook food using high-heat cooking methods, like deep frying in oil, it releases dangerous compounds like acrylamide. A study published by the International Agency for Research on Cancer has revealed that exposure to acrylamide can elevate the risk of some cancers, especially endometrial, pancreatic, breast, ovarian, and esophageal cancers. [4] Research has also provided evidence proving the link between the dietary intake of acrylamide and the risk of kidney dysfunction including kidney cancer. [5] You can avoid these health risks by switching to air frying, which is considered a healthier way to cook food because it inhibits the release of acrylamide in the food. [6]

CRISP & CRUNCHY DISHES

If you love to eat frozen or breaded foods, such as chicken tenders and onion rings, you will also love having them cooked in an air fryer. The air fryers actually crisp up the food, giving them a golden and crunchy exterior, instead of a soggy mess. You just have to spray a very small quantity of healthy cooking oils like olive oil on the outside of the food to get that crispy and crunchy exterior you love.

HIGHLY VERSATILE

Air fryers are much more than just healthier alternatives to deep frying. Actually, most people are under the impression that air fryers can be used only for preparing dishes that involve deep drying. But this is not true. The fact is that you can use it to cook virtually anything from French fries, whole spaghetti squash, and fried chicken, to curries and desserts. Air fryers are also great for cooking other store-bought frozen foods like pizza rolls and tater tots. And it's so easy that even kids can use it.

SAFETY

Air fryers are considered safer than deep fryers because deep-frying involves heating the food in a large container full of hot scalding oil. This could pose a safety risk. Air fryers, on the other hand, do not involve risks like splashing or spilling oil or touching hot oil accidentally. Following the proper instructions for using this appliance can reduce potential risks, making it a safer choice.

CONVENIENCE

Air fryers offer a higher convenience than the traditional methods of cooking because they are faster and easier to use. An air fryer makes cooking meals more exciting and less complicated. All you need to do is marinate or season a piece of chicken breast or any other meat of your choice, place it in the fryer, and set it to cook.

FASTER COOKING

Another major advantage of air fryers is that these appliances get extremely hot much faster than ovens. The circulating hot air ensures the food is cooked evenly and gets crispy and browned, all without much intervention from you. This can allow you to cut down your cooking time significantly.

EASY REHEATING

You can use your air fryer even for reheating food. There are many reasons why you might want to reheat food using an air fryer. For instance, it offers an easy and quick way to reheat food. It also keeps food from burning or overcooking. Moreover, it keeps the food tasting fresh and crispy.

EASY TO CLEAN

Cleaning up later is often the most difficult and annoying part of cooking. It is such an unpleasant task that it can wipe away a great deal of excitement from a nice meal. That is what makes air fryers a delightful way to cook meals. Air fryers are incredibly easy to clean after cooking. Unlike deep-drying, air fryers do not create a lot of mess and so it takes very little time and effort to clean up.

These benefits make air fryers a great appliance to use in your kitchen on a daily basis. Cooking with an air fryer is going to get even more exciting when we start learning some of the best but easy recipes for breakfast, lunch, and dinner.

But before that, let's first answer some common questions people often have about air fryers. This will give you a better idea of how to put your appliance to the best use when we start with the recipes.

COOKING WITH AIR FRYERS FREQUENTLY ASKED QUESTIONS

DO I NEED TO PREHEAT AIR FRYER?

Yes, although not a mandatory practice, it is best to preheat the air fryer before you place food into it simply because it can reduce your total cooking time. But, unlike ovens, air fryers do not require preheating a whole half hour beforehand to get to the required temperature. A few minutes of preheating is often enough.

One more thing... If you are ready to place the food into the air fryer and realise that you forgot to preheat it, then you need not wait for it to be preheated. You can simply place the food into the fryer and set the temperature. As I said before, preheating is not mandatory but does come with some benefits.
Some models of air fryers have an indicator that shows when the unit is adequately preheated.

HOW DO I REHEAT FOOD IN AN AIR FRYER?

Air fryers offer an easy and convenient way to reheat foods. It can also crisp them back up. It takes just a few minutes to reheat food in an air fryer. For reheating, you can set your fryer at a temperature that is approximately 30 degrees lower than the temperature at which you usually set your air fry for cooking that food.

WHICH OIL IS THE BEST TO USE IN AN AIR FRYER?

You can use extra virgin olive oil, canola oil, or avocado oil. These oils offer a good source of healthy fats like omega-3 fatty acids. Studies have shown that omega-3s can improve your cholesterol levels and reduce the risk of heart disease. Cooking in these oils is also an effective way to avoid diabetes and obesity. [7] [8]

WHAT SIZE DO I NEED?

Usually, an air fryer with a capacity of 1.75 to 3 litres is suitable for preparing meals for two to three people. You can choose an air fryer with a larger capacity if your family comprises more than three people. Also, remember that large air fryers with a capacity of four to five litres may sometimes need you to cook in batches depending on the recipe.

HOW DO I CLEAN AIR FRYER?

It is very important to clean your air fryer after each use to ensure your appliance lasts longer and works as efficiently as expected. Also, not cleaning it regularly will lead to the build-up of oil in the unit making it smoke.

You can clean the air fryer by gently wiping off the basket or shelf using a paper towel. If it feels or appears gunky, you can take it out and wash it using your regular soap and water. You can clean the shelf or basket in a dishwasher if it is dishwasher safe.

WHAT ARE THE SAFETY PRECAUTIONS I NEED TO FOLLOW?

- Carefully read and follow all the safety precautions included in the air fryer's manual.
- Wear gloves while checking or taking out food from the fryer. You can use a potholder to hold the basket to avoid scalding your skin.
- Never fill the air fryer basket with oil. Remember that an air fryer is designed to be used for air frying, not oil frying.
- Check the smoking point of the food you are cooking. It's best to set the temperature lower than the smoke point to prevent the food from burning or smoking.
- Avoid using oils having a low smoke point to ensure the oil does not burn, smoke, or splatter on the heating elements of the fryer.
- Cook in a well-ventilated area. Make sure there is plenty of space around the fryer to allow the exhaust to ventilate. Avoid keeping it too close to a wall.
- Always unplug the fryer when not in use.
- Never place your air fryer on the stove.

Owning an air fryer is one of the best decisions you can make to ensure the meals you prepare are healthy and delicious. It can also save cooking time and reduce the effort in clean-up.

We will now start learning all kinds of tasty and tempting dishes you can prepare using your air fryer. Try these dishes to make cooking less tedious and your meals more exciting!

Please scan the QR code below to access your bonus PDF with all 150 recipes with full coloured photos & beautiful designs alongside! This is the only way we can get the recipes with coloured photos to you & keep the book as reasonably priced as possible.

Also, once downloaded you can take the PDF with you digitally wherever you go- meaning you can cook these recipes wherever you may be! (As long as you have an air fryer!)

We hope you enjoy and do let us know your feedback!

STEP BY STEP Guide To Access-

1. Open Your Phones (Or Any Device You Want The Book On) Back Camera. The Back Camera Is The One You use as if you are taking a picture of someone.
2. Simply point your Camera at the QR code and 'tap' the QR code with your finger to focus the camera.
3. A link / pop up will appear. Simply tap that (and make sure you have internet connection) and the
4. FREE PDF containing all of the coloured images should appear.
5. Now you have access to these FOREVER. Simply 'Bookmark' The tab it opened on, or download the document and take wherever you want.
6. Repeat this on any device you want it on! (If you want it on a laptop, simply email the document to yourself!)
7. Any issues please email us at *vicandersonpublishing@gmail.com* and we will be happy to help!!

SECTION 1

VEGAN RECIPES

01. PORTOBELLO MUSHROOM PIZZA

- If you love mushrooms, this recipe is just what you are looking for. These personal "pizzas" can make up for a great appetizer as well as your mid-meal snack.
- Preparation Time: 15 minutes
- Cooking Time: 10 minutes

Servings: 4

Per serving:

Kcal: 300; Fat: 36g; Carbs: 35g; Protein: 36g; Sugars: 10g; Fibre: 8g

Ingredients:

- 4 portobello mushrooms
- 1 tsp. balsamic vinegar
- 4 tsp. oil-free pasta sauce
- 100g hummus
- 100g courgette shredded and chopped
- 2 tsp. sweet red pepper diced
- 1 clove garlic, minced
- 4 olives, sliced
- 1 tsp. dried basil
- 1 bunch basil leaves, minced
- 1 tsp. salt
- ½ tsp. black pepper

Instructions:

- Step 1: Wash the portobellos and cut off the stems. Remove the gills gently with a blunt spoon. Pat dry the insides. Bush both sides with very little balsamic vinegar. And a sprinkle of salt and pepper.
- Step 2: Spread pasta sauce inside each mushroom and sprinkle garlic.
- Step 3: Preheat the air fryer to 176°C. Place mushrooms on a shelf of the fryer in a single layer and air fry for 3 minutes
- Step 4: Remove mushrooms from the fryer and top each one with courgette, peppers, and olives. Sprinkle dried basil and salt and pepper.
- Step 5: Return the mushroom to the fryer and cook for another 3 minutes.
- Step 6: Remove, and place on a plate. Drizzle with hummus and sprinkle basil.

02. TOFU SCRAMBLE

- Tofu scramble is a good recipe to eat for your breakfast, lunch, and dinner. It provides a good source of protein as well as omega-3 fatty acids that will keep you fit and healthy.
- Preparation Time: 5 minutes
- Cooking Time: 30 minutes

Servings: 4

Per serving:

Kcal: 274; Fat: 25g; Carbs: 45g; Protein: 28g; Sugars: 4g; Fibre: 8g

Ingredients:

- 1 block tofu, chopped into 2-cm pieces
- 2 tsp. soy sauce
- 1 tsp. turmeric
- 1 tsp. garlic powder
- 1 chopped onion
- 1 tsp. onion powder
- 2 red potatoes, peeled and cubed
- 1 tsp. olive oil
- 4 broccoli florets
- 1 tsp. olive oil

Instructions:

- Step 1: Toss together the tofu, olive oil, turmeric, soy sauce, garlic powder, onion powder, and onion in a medium-sized bowl. Set aside to marinate.
- Step 2: In another bowl, toss the potatoes in olive oil and air fry for 15 minutes at 176°C, shaking once around 6 to 8 minutes into cooking.
- Step 3: Shake the potatoes again. Add the tofu, reserving the leftover marinade. Set the potatoes and tofu to cook for 15 more minutes.
- Step 4: While the tofu is cooking, add the broccoli to the remaining marinade. When 5 minutes of cooking time is left, add the broccoli to the air fryer.
- Step 5: Remove and serve hot.

03. CRUNCH TORTILLA WRAPS

- This crunch tortilla wrap is a tempting plant-based vegan dinner recipe that is super easy and quick to make. It also packs a punch of protein and gives a boost of energy.
- **Preparation Time**: 5 minutes
- **Cooking Time**: 8 minutes
- **Servings**: 4

Servings: 4

Per serving:

Kcal: 510; Fat: 27g; Carbs: 56g; **Protein**: 20g; Sugars: 2.8g; Fibre: 10g

Ingredients:

- 1 regular-size tortilla wrap
- 2 tsp. grated vegan cheese
- 2 tsp. refried pinto beans
- 2 iceberg lettuce leaves
- 1 small corn tortilla wraps
- 2 tsp. guacamole
- 2 tsp. salsa

Instructions:

- Step 1: Preheat the air fryer to 176 C.
- Step 2: Assemble the crunch tortilla wraps by stacking each in this order: large regular tortilla wraps, beans, grated cheese, small corn tortilla wraps, salsa, whole iceberg lettuce leaves, and finally, guacamole.
- Step 3: Fold the tortilla wraps, turn them gently, and fold and turn again.
- Step 4: Add some more cheese to 'seal' and close each tortilla wrap.
- Step 5: Place the tortilla wraps in the air fryer and bake for 6 minutes at 176 C.
- Step 6: Serve with guacamole or dairy-free sour cream for dipping.

04. SMOKY CHICKPEAS

- This recipe gives you a great way to up your snacking game. They are quick, easy to prepare, and also healthy.
- Preparation Time: 5 minutes
- **Cooking Time:** 18 minutes

Servings: 4

Per serving:

Kcal: 260; Fat: 25g; Carbs: 45g; Protein: 26g; Sugars: 3g; Fibre: 8g

Ingredients:

- One can chickpeas, thoroughly rinsed and drained
- 1 tsp. sunflower oil
- 1 tsp. lemon juice
- 1 tsp. smoked paprika
- ½ tsp. ground cumin
- ½ tsp. granulated garlic
- ½ tsp. granulated onion
- ½ tsp. of salt, more to taste
- ½ tsp. of pepper

Instructions:

- Step 1: Set your air fryer to 176 C.
- Step 2: Place the chickpeas in the basket of the air fryer and fry for about 10 minutes or until they are dry. Shake the basket once at the midway mark.
- Step 3: Meanwhile, prepare the seasoning. Add the lemon, oil, and all seasonings in a medium bowl and whisk to combine well.
- Step 4: Add the fried chickpeas carefully to the bowl of seasonings and stir to combine well.
- Step 5: Place the seasoned chickpeas in the air fryer basket and set it to 176 C.
- Step 6: Fry for 2 to 3 minutes until the desired crispiness is reached. Shake the basket once at the midway mark.

05. POPCORN TOFU

- This Popcorn Tofu is delicious crispy, and dippable. It is a great alternative to deep-fried nuggets. You can try this dish when you're in the mood to eat fast-food that is also healthy.
- **Preparation Time:** 15 minutes
- **Cooking Time:** 12 minutes

Servings: 4

Per serving:

260; Fat: 11g; Carbs: 37g; Protein: 16g; Sugars: 2.6g; Fibre: 6g

Ingredients:

- 100g tofu in water, drained and pressed
- 100g quinoa flour
- 50g cornmeal
- 1 tsp. Dijon mustard
- 2 tsp. onion powder
- 2 tsp. garlic powder
- 3 tsp. nutritional yeast
- 1 tsp. pepper
- 1 tsp. salt
- 50ml dairy-free milk
- 50g panko breadcrumbs
- 2 tsp. Sriracha Mayo
- 10ml vegan mayo

Instructions:

- Step 1: Cut the pressed tofu into small bite-size pieces.
- Step 2: Add cornmeal, flour, nutritional yeast, mustard, onion, salt, garlic, pepper, and milk into a bowl and mix to combine well. Add milk if needed to thin it out. The consistency should be like that of pancake batter.
- Step 3: Add breadcrumbs to another bowl.
- Step 4: Dip the pieces of tofu into the batter, and then into breadcrumbs.
- Step 5: Place the nuggets into the air fryer basket. Set the air fryer to 176 C and cook for 12 minutes. Shake the basket gently halfway through.
- Step 6: Mix sriracha and vegan mayo together and serve with popcorn tofu.

06. FRIED RICE

- Fried rice is an easy and quick air fryer recipe that will make your tummy happy and full without the hassle of extra oil!
- Preparation Time: 5 minutes
- Cooking Time: 15 minutes

Servings: 4

Per serving:

Kcal: 520; Fat: 48g; Carbs: 60g; Protein: 28g; Sugars: 8g; Fibre: 7g

Ingredients:

- 150g rice, cooked
- 200g mixed vegetables like carrots, broccoli, and corn
- 10g coconut aminos
- 1 tsp. oil

Instructions:

- Step 1: Put the cooked rice into a large bowl. Add the vegetables, coconut aminos, and oil to the bowl and mix until well combined.
- Step 2: Transfer the rice mixture to the air fryer basket and cook for 15 minutes at 190 C, stirring 3 times through the cooking period.

07. NUT-FREE, SOY-FREE BROWNIES

- These Nut-Free, Soy-Free Brownies are sure to satisfy your craving for a dessert. These are also specifically suited for those having an allergy to nuts.
- Preparation Time: 10 minutes
- Cooking Time: 20 minutes

Servings: 4

Per serving:

Kcal: 220; Fat: 8g; Carbs: 41g; Protein: 4g; Sugars: 25g; Fibre: 5g

Ingredients:

DRY INGREDIENTS

- 100g whole wheat pastry flour
- 50g vegan sugar
- 1 tsp. ground flax seeds
- 4 to 5 tbsp. cocoa powder
- ½ tsp. salt

WET INGREDIENTS

- 50ml non-dairy milk
- 50ml aquafaba
- ½ tsp. vanilla extract

Instructions:

- Step 1: Mix the wet ingredients in a bowl. Then, mix the dry ingredients in another bowl. Add the dry ingredients to the wet ingredients in a large bowl and mix well.
- Step 2: Preheat the air fryer to 176 C.
- Step 3: Spray some oil onto the pan and transfer the contents from the large bowl to the pan. Shake gently to spread it evenly.
- Step 4: Place the pan in the air fryer basket and cook for 20 minutes.

08. KALE AND POTATO NUGGETS

- These Kale and Potato bites are nutritious and tasty! This recipe offers a great way to use your leftover mashed potatoes to prepare a side dish for your lunch and dinner. So, you can just skip the steps for cooking the potatoes and use our leftover mashers instead.
- **Preparation Time:** 10 minutes
- **Cooking Time:** 20 minutes

Servings: 4
Per serving:

Kcal: 290; Fat: 21g; Carbs: 35g; Protein: 29g; Sugars: 6g; Fibre: 6g

Ingredients:

- 2 potatoes, finely chopped
- 1 or 2 cloves garlic, minced
- 1 tsp. canola oil or extra-virgin olive oil
- 2 bunches kale, coarsely chopped
- 50ml almond milk
- 1 tsp. salt
- ½ tsp. black pepper

Instructions:

- Step 1: Add the potatoes to a saucepan of boiling water and cook until tender.
- Step 2: In a skillet, heat the oil over medium heat. Add garlic cloves and sauté until golden brown. Add kale and sauté for another 2 to 3 minutes. Transfer the contents to a large bowl.
- Step 3: Drain the cooked potatoes. Transfer them to a bowl. Add milk, pepper, and salt, and mash well. Transfer to the large bowl and add the garlic and cooked kale.
- Step 4: Preheat the air fryer to 176 C for 5 minutes.
- Step 5: Roll the kale and potato mixture into small 2.5-cm nuggets. Spritz the basket of your air fryer with very little vegetable oil. Place the nuggets in the fryer and cook for 10 to 15 minutes, shaking at 6 minutes.

09. HEALTHY FRENCH FRIES

- These healthy fries prepared in your air fryer using minimal oil will make a no-guilt alternative to your French fries!
- **Preparation Time:** 10 minutes
- **Cooking Time:** 25 minutes

Servings: 4

Per serving:

Kcal: 400; Fat: 50g; Carbs: 45g; Protein: 28g; Sugars: 13g; Fibre: 18g

Ingredients:

- 3 medium potatoes
- 1 tsp. onion powder
- 1 tsp. garlic powder
- ¼ tsp. basil
- ¼ tsp. paprika
- ¼ tsp. chili powder
- Salt to taste

Instructions:

- Step 1: Peel the potatoes and rinse them well.
- Step 2: Slice them into the shape of fries.
- Step 3: Toss the fries with the onion powder, garlic powder, and the remaining ingredients.
- Step 4: Put the fries into the air fryer basket and fry at 189 C for 20 to 25 minutes, stirring every 5 minutes.
- Step 5: Serve with the dip of your choice.

10. NUTTY FRENCH TOAST

- This recipe topped with crispy oats and crunchy pecans can make up for the low protein content of plant-based diets that most vegans worry about. You can cut the bread into wedges and fingers to make them more fun to eat!
- **Preparation Time:** 10 minutes
- **Cooking Time:** 6 minute

Servings: 4

Per serving:

Kcal: 250; Fat: 25g; Carbs: 35g; Protein: 20g; Sugars: 8g; Fibre: 10g

Ingredients:

- 8 slices of whole grain bread
- 100g rolled oats
- 50g pecans
- 2 tsp. ground flax seed
- 1 tsp. ground cinnamon
- 50ml non-dairy milk
- 1 tsp. maple syrup

Instructions:

- Step 1: To prepare the topping, add the oats, cinnamon, nuts, and flax seeds to your food processor. Pulse until it looks like breadcrumbs. Pour into a wide pan.
- Step 2: Add the non-dairy milk to another container, and soak one or two slices of the bread in it for about 15 seconds. Turn and soak the other side.
- Step 3: Place the slices into the air fryer basket in a single layer without overlapping.
- Step 4: Cook for 3 minutes at 176 C, then flip the bread. Cook for 3 more minutes.
- Step 5: Top with maple syrup and serve.

11. SPICED KALE CHIPS

- These light and crispy spiced chips will delicately spice up your meals and satisfy your cravings for fast food.
- **Preparation time:** 5 minutes
- **Cooking time:** 20 minutes

Servings: 4

Per serving:

Kcal: 290; Fat: 29g; Carbs: 40g; Protein: 24g; Sugars: 8g; Fibre: 9g

Ingredients:

- 1 large bunch kale, washed and chopped
- 1 tbsp. olive oil
- 1 or 2 tbsp. seasoning of your choice
- 1 tsp. sea salt

Instructions:

- Step 1: Place the washed and dried kale into a mixing bowl and drizzle with olive oil.
- Step 2: Massage the olive oil into the kale gently using your hands, until well coated.
- Step 3: Add seasonings and toss well
- Step 4: Place kale in the basket of your air fryer and cook for 5 minutes at 170 C. Your chips should be ready when the edges turn brown but are not burned.

12. BAKED APPLE

This one's a quick recipe that will hardly need any preparation. Additionally, it will provide a good source of iron and several vitamins and minerals.

Preparation Time: 5 minutes

Cooking Time: 10 minutes

Servings: 4

Per serving:

Kcal: 150; Fat: 8g; Carbs: 25g; Protein: 12g; Sugars: 11g; Fibre: 12

Ingredients:

- 4 apples
- 2 tbsp. chopped walnuts
- 2 tbsp. raisins
- 1 tsp. light margarine, melted
- ½ tsp. cinnamon
- ½ tsp. nutmeg
- 50ml water

Instructions:

- Step 1: Preheat the air fryer to 176 C.
- Step 2: Cut each apple in half around the middle. Spoon out some of the flesh.
- Step 3: In a small bowl, combine cinnamon, nutmeg, margarine, walnuts, and raisins.
- Step 4: Spoon this mixture into the centre of the halves of the apples.
- Step 5: Place the apples in the basket of the air fryer. Bake for 10 minutes and serve.

13. REUBEN ROLLS

- Reuben rolls are a gluten-free vegan option for all those who love to have desserts after meals. It is easy to digest and contains less calories, making it a good option even for diabetic patients and those trying to lose weight.
- **Preparation Time:** 15 minutes
- **Cooking Time:** 15 minutes

Servings: 4

Per serving:

Kcal: 200; Fat: 27g; Carbs: 25g; Protein: 21g; Sugars: 6g; Fibre: 6g

Ingredients:

- 1 small jackfruit, cut into small chunks
- 2 tsp. vegan mayonnaise
- 2 sweet onions, peeled and diced
- 2 garlic cloves, peeled and minced
- 6 to 8 slices vegan cheese
- 2 dill pickles, finely chopped
- 12 vegan rice tortilla wraps

Instructions:

- Step 1: Combine the jackfruit chunks and the mayonnaise or any other vegan dressing of your choice. Set aside to marinate.
- Step 2: In a saucepan, sauté onion and garlic over medium heat. Remove from heat and combine with the jackfruit mixture.
- Step 3: To assemble rolls: arrange each rice tortilla wrap in a diamond shape. Place 2 tablespoons of jackfruit mixture in the bottom corner of the wraps. Top with half a cheese slice and one tablespoon of pickles. Roll each tortilla wrap gently.
- Step 4: Brush each roll with pickle juice lightly.
- Step 5: Place them in the air fryer in a single layer without overlapping and cook for 5 minutes at 176 C.
- Step 6: Remove and turn the rolls. Cook for another 3 minutes, or until they become crisp and golden brown.

14. VEGETABLE BIRYANI

- This Indian delicacy comes with a rich supply of complex carbs, vitamins, minerals, and several other nutrients. This recipe is highly filling and can be your standalone dish for lunch or dinner.
- **Preparation Time**: 5 minutes
- **Cooking Time**: 15 minuteS

Servings: 4

Per serving:

Kcal: 520; Fat: 48g; Carbs: 60g; Protein: 28g; Sugars: 8g; Fibre: 7g

Ingredients:

- 100g basmati rice
- 1 onion, chopped
- 1 bell pepper, sliced
- 5 mushrooms, sliced
- 2 carrots, chopped
- 1 tbsp. ground coriander seeds
- 1 tbsp. cumin seeds
- 1 tsp. turmeric
- 1 tbsp. green chilies, chopped
- 1 tbsp. red chili powder
- 1 tbsp. ginger paste
- 1 tbsp. garlic paste
- Salt and pepper to taste
- Coriander to garnish

Instructions:

- Step 1: Boil the basmati rice in water for 10 minutes. Drain the rice and set aside.
- Step 2: Add chopped onions, green chilies, cumin seeds, ginger, and garlic paste to a pan and allow to caramelize in very little oil. Add the chopped vegetables and mix well. Add the salt and pepper. Once the vegetables are soft, take them off the heat and set aside.
- Step 3: In an air fryer basket, add one layer of cooked basmati rice. Then, add one thin layer of the vegetable mixture. Continue doing this until both the rice and the mixture are used up.
- Step 4: Cook in your air fryer for 15 minutes at 180°C. Garnish with coriander and serve.

15. CRUMBLE WITH PEAR AND BLUEBERRIES

- This delicious recipe is rich in vitamin C, fibre, and other vital nutrients that the body needs to strengthen your immunity and digestion.
- **Preparation Time:** 15 minutes
- **Cooking Time:** 15 minutes

Servings: 4

Per serving:

Kcal: 280; Fat: 20g; Carbs: 30g; Protein: 26g; Sugars: 7g; Fibre: 7g

Ingredients:

- 4 pears, finely diced
- 100g blueberries
- 100g rice flour
- 2 tsp. sugar
- ½ tsp. ground cinnamon
- 2 tsp. non-dairy butter

Instructions:

Step 1: Preheat your air fryer to 176 C for 5 minutes. Combine the pear and blueberries in an air fryer–safe pan.

Step 2: In a small bowl, combine sugar, flour, cinnamon, and butter. Spoon the mixture over the fruits. Sprinkle a little extra flour to cover any exposed fruit.

Step 3: Cook at 176 C for 15 minutes and serve.

16. SPICY CAULIFLOWER STIR-FRIES

- These air-fried cauliflower stir-fries are tempting and irresistible. They are fast and simple to prepare for your lunch and dinner and need very little effort.
- **Preparation Time:** 5 minutes
- **Cooking Time:** 20 minutes

Servings: 4

Per serving:

Kcal: 270; Fat: 37g; Carbs: 35g; Protein: 25g; Sugars: 8g; Fibre: 7g

Ingredients:

- 2 cauliflowers, cut into small florets
- 1 onion, thinly sliced
- 5 garlic cloves, finely sliced
- 1 tsp. rice vinegar
- 1 tsp. coconut sugar
- 1 tsp. hot sauce of your choice
- 2 scallions
- 1 tsp. salt
- 1 tsp. black pepper

Instructions:

Step 1: Place cauliflower florets in the air fryer and cook for 10 minutes at 176 C.

Step 2: Open the air fryer, add the sliced onion and finely chopped garlic, and stir well. Cook for another 10 minutes.

Step 3: Mix rice vinegar, coconut sugar, hot sauce, salt, and pepper in a small bowl.

Step 4: Add the mixture to the cauliflower florets and stir well. Cook for 5 more minutes.

Step 5: Sprinkle the sliced scallions over the florets to garnish. Serve hot.

17. PEANUT BANANA DESSERT

- This low-calorie dessert recipe contains a lesser amount of sugar but a good amount of protein. Good recipe to try to please your sweet tooth without compromising on your calorie intake while on a weight loss diet.
- Preparation Time: 15 minutes
- Cooking Time: 6 minutes

Servings: 4
Per serving:

Kcal: 200; Fat: 27g; Carbs: 25g; Protein: 21g; Sugars: 6g; Fibre: 6g

Ingredients:

- 1 large banana (sliced)
- 12 rice or whole-wheat tortilla wraps
- 3 to 4 tbsp. peanut butter
- 1 tsp. coconut or avocado oil
- 1 tsp. vegan chocolate chips
- 1 tsp. raisins
- 1 tsp. ground cinnamon

Instructions:

Step 1: Slice the banana and place the pieces in a bowl of water. Add a splash of lemon juice to prevent the banana from browning.

Step 2: Place one slice on each tortilla wrap and add 1 teaspoon of peanut butter on top of it. Brush water along the edges of the tortilla wraps and bring together the opposite corners. Squeeze gently to close the edges. Fold up the remaining opposite sides and squeeze gently.

Step 3: Place the tortilla wraps in the air fryer basket and spray generously with coconut or avocado oil.

Step 4: Cook for 5 to 6 minutes at 180 C.

Step 5: Serve with a scoop of ice cream and sprinkle raisins, chocolate chips, and cinnamon.

18. PULLED VEGAN PORK

- This dish has a great texture. It contains coconut milk, which is a good source of MCTs (medium chain triglycerides) that can help promote weight loss.
- **Preparation Time:** 13 minutes
- **Cooking Time:** 8 minutes

Servings: 4

Per serving:

Kcal: 140; Fat: 17g; Carbs: 15g; Protein: 26g; Sugars: 6g; Fibre: 7g

Ingredients:

- 100g Soy Mince & Soya protein
- 1 tsp. vegan mayonnaise
- 25ml vegan BBQ sauce
- 1 tsp. canola oil
- 4 to 5 tbsp. grated coconut
- 50ml warm water

Instructions:

Step 1: Soak the Soy Mince & Soya protein pieces in water for 10 minutes and drain. Mix well with mayonnaise.

Step 2: Move the contents to another bowl and pull apart the hydrated protein pieces into thin shreds, like shredding string cheese.

Step 3: Add to the air fryer basket and cook for 3 minutes at 176 C.

Step 4: Remove them from the fryer and transfer them back to the bowl.

Step 5: Toss in BBQ sauce and stir well. Make sure all the protein pieces are evenly coated.

Step 6: Return to the air fryer and cook for another 2 to 3 minutes, stopping twice to shake the pan.

19. CRUMBLE WITH APPLE AND STRAWBERRIES

- This delicious recipe will provide loads of nutrition from berries and apples together with natural plant-based antioxidants that your body needs to fight infections and inflammation.
- **Preparation Time:** 15 minutes
- **Cooking Time:** 15 minutes

Servings: 4

Per serving:

Kcal: 310; Fat: 20g; Carbs: 40g; Protein: 28g; Sugars: 8g; Fibre: 7g

Ingredients:

- 1 apple, finely diced
- 100g frozen strawberries
- 50g brown rice flour
- 2 tsp. sugar
- ½ tsp. ground cinnamon
- 2 tsp. non-dairy butter

Instructions:

Step 1: Preheat your air fryer to 176 C for 5 minutes. Combine the apple and frozen or fresh strawberries in an air fryer–safe pan.

Step 2: In a small bowl, combine sugar, flour, cinnamon, and butter. Spoon the mixture over the fruits. Sprinkle a little extra flour to cover any exposed fruit.

Step 3: Cook at 176 C for 15 minutes.

20. BAKED PEARS

- Pears offer a rich source of several essential minerals that the body needs to support metabolic processes. This recipe is also tasty and very simple to prepare, making it a good option to prepare for your breakfast or even to relieve your mid-meal hunger pangs.
- **Preparation Time:** 5 minutes
- **Cooking Time:** 10 minutes

Servings: 4

Per serving:

Kcal: 260; Fat: 25g; Carbs: 45g; Protein: 26g; Sugars: 3g; Fibre: 8g

Ingredients:

- 4 pears
- 2 tbsp. chopped almonds
- 2 tbsp. raisins
- 1 tsp. margarine, melted
- ½ tsp. cinnamon powder
- ½ tsp. nutmeg powder

Instructions:

Step 1: Preheat the air fryer to 176 C.

Step 2: Cut the pear in half around the middle. Spoon out some of the flesh.

Step 3: In a small bowl, combine cinnamon, nutmeg, margarine, almonds, and raisins.

Step 4: Spoon this mixture into the centre of the halves of the pear.

Step 5: Place the pear in the basket of the air fryer.

Step 6: Bake for 20 minutes.

Please scan the QR code below to access your bonus PDF with all 150 recipes with full coloured photos & beautiful designs alongside! This is the only way we can get the recipes with coloured photos to you & keep the book as reasonably priced as possible.

Also, once downloaded you can take the PDF with you digitally wherever you go- meaning you can cook these recipes wherever you may be! (As long as you have an air fryer!)

We hope you enjoy and do let us know your feedback!

STEP BY STEP Guide To Access-

1. Open Your Phones (Or Any Device You Want The Book On) Back Camera. The Back Camera Is The One You use as if you are taking a picture of someone.
2. Simply point your Camera at the QR code and 'tap' the QR code with your finger to focus the camera.
3. A link / pop up will appear. Simply tap that (and make sure you have internet connection) and the
4. FREE PDF containing all of the coloured images should appear.
5. Now you have access to these FOREVER. Simply 'Bookmark' The tab it opened on, or download the document and take wherever you want.
6. Repeat this on any device you want it on! (If you want it on a laptop, simply email the document to yourself!)
7. Any issues please email us at *vicandersonpublishing@gmail.com* and we will be happy to help!!

02

SECTION 2

BREAKFAST

01 PROTEIN RICH GRANOLA

- This air fryer granola recipe makes granola even more healthy. It provides a rich source of fibre that can improve digestion and promote bowel movements. This dish also has healthy ingredients like nuts and seeds that are loaded with protein and omega-3 fatty acids.
- **Preparation Time:** 5 minutes
- **Cooking Time:** 15 minutes

Servings: 4

Per serving:

Kcal: 360; Fat: 35g; Carbs: 65g; Protein: 36g; Sugars: 10g; Fibre: 15g

Ingredients:

- 100g rolled oats
- 50g dried cherries
- 50g dried cranberries
- 50g toasted wheat germ
- 20g dried blueberries
- 1 tsp. flaxseed
- 1 tsp. sunflower seeds
- 1 tsp. chopped pecans
- 1 tsp. chopped almonds
- 2 tsp. chopped walnuts

- 2 tsp. chopped hazelnuts
- 1 tsp. vanilla extract
- 2 tsp. honey or agave extract
- 6 tsp. olive oil
- 5ml maple syrup
- 1 tsp. ground cinnamon

Instructions:

- Step 1: Mix the dry ingredient in an air fryer-safe bowl.
- Step 2: Mix the agave or honey with maple syrup and oil. Mix dry ingredients with this syrup mix, stirring well to coat all of the ingredients fully.
- Step 3: Preheat the air fryer to 176 C.
- Step 4: Place the bowl in the air fryer. Cook for 15 minutes, stirring every 5 minutes or until the granola turns golden brown.
- Allow to cool and serve.

02 STRAWBERRY POP TARTS

- Strawberry pop tarts are perfect to satisfy your craving for sugar. This is a great recipe to begin your day on an energetic note, especially when you know you are going to need a lot of energy that day!
- **Preparation Time:** 10 minutes
- **Cooking Time:** 11 minutes

Servings: 4

Per serving:

Kcal: 380; Fat: 37g; Carbs: 67g; Protein: 38g; Sugars: 12g; Fibre: 17g

Ingredients:

- 1kg refrigerated pie crusts
- 6 tsp. strawberry jam
- 2 tsp. heavy cream
- 4 tsp. powdered sugar
- 1 tsp. vanilla extract
- 2 tsp. melted butter
- Sprinkles of your choice

Instructions:

- Step 1: Remove the pie crusts from the refrigerator at least 15 minutes before you want to start cooking. Cut the crusts into 4 rectangles. Then, combine the remaining dough, and re-roll it out. Cut 4 more rectangles out of it.
- Step 2: Place strawberry jam in the centre of each rectangle.
- Step 3: Spread out the jam to within ½ cm of the edge of the pie.
- Step 4: Moisten the outer side of each pie crust round with very little water using your finger.
- Step 5: Place another pastry rectangle on each filling rectangle.
- Step 6: Press the seams together using your fingers and crimp the edges together using a fork.
- Step 7: Preheat the air fryer to 176 C and set the timer to 11 minutes.
- Step 8: Place the pop-tarts into the basket and allow to cook. Once cooked, allow cooling completely before frosting.
-
- Step 9: Whisk together powdered sugar, butter, heavy cream, and vanilla extract in a small bowl, until they are well combined.
- Step 10: Spread the frosting on the cooled tarts and sprinkle the sprinkles. Let the frosting become a bit hard in the fridge before serving.

03 FRENCH TOAST

- French toast is the perfect way to start your day with a healthy dose of protein. It is delicious and very simple, to prepare.
- **Preparation Time:** 5 minutes
- **Cooking Time:** 9 minutes

Servings: 4

Per serving:

Kcal: 190; Fat: 15g; Carbs: 35g; Protein: 16g; Sugars:7g; Fibre: 6g

Ingredients:

- 2 eggs
- 1 loaf brioche or challah bread, cut into 8 slices
- 2 tsp. milk
- ½ tsp. vanilla extract
- ½ tsp. ground cinnamon

Instructions:

- Step 1: Add milk, egg, vanilla, and cinnamon in a medium bowl, and whisk to combine well. Set it aside.
- Step 2: Set up the whisked egg mixture and the slices of bread next to each other.
- Step 3: Spray the basket of the air fryer with non-stick oil spray.
- Step 4: Now, gently dip the slices of bread into the mixture while flipping to coat both sides. Lift each slice out of the mixture and wait for a few seconds to allow it to drip, and then, place it into the basket. Repeat for all slices
- Step 5: Set the air fryer to 176 C and allow it to cook for 5 minutes.
- Open the basket and flip each French toast slice carefully. Cook for another 3 to 4 minutes.
- Step 6: Serve immediately with warm maple syrup or powdered sugar.

04 ROASTED POTATOES

- Breakfast Potatoes are crispy on the outside and creamy on the inside. Cooked with fast-circulating hot air in an air freer, this recipe takes very little time and needs a minimal amount of oil.
- **Preparation Time:** 2 minutes
- **Cooking Time:** 15 minutes

Servings: 4

Per serving:

Kcal: 190; Fat: 15g; Carbs: 35g; Protein: 16g; Sugars:7g; Fibre: 6g

Ingredients:

- 5 medium potatoes
- 1 tbsp. olive oil
- Seasoning of your choice
- ½ tsp. kosher salt
- ½ tsp. black ground pepper
- ½ tsp. smoked paprika
- ½ tsp. garlic powder

Instructions:

- Step 1: Preheat the air fryer to 176 C for about 2 to 3 minutes.
- Step 2: Peel and cut the potatoes into small cubes.
- Step 3: Toss the potatoes with seasoning and oil, and make sure all the potato cubes are thoroughly coated.
- Step 4: Spray the air fryer basket with a non-stick spray and place the potatoes in it.
- Step 5: Cook for about 15 minutes. Stop and shake the basket 2 to 3 times throughout to ensure even cooking.
- Step 6: Transfer to a plate and serve immediately.

05 SWEET SAUSAGE

- Sweet Sausage can be a perfect recipe to start your day on an energetic note. It is filled with proteins and other nutrients. It has the perfect texture and taste that will satisfy your taste buds.
- **Preparation Time:** 10 minutes
- **Cooking Time: 15** minutes

Servings: 4
Per serving:

Kcal: 280; Fat: 23g; Carbs: 34g; Protein: 11g; Sugars: 8g; Fibre: 7g

Ingredients:

- 1kg ground pork
- ¼ tsp. dried oregano
- ¼ tsp. dried rosemary
- 3 tbsp. minced fresh parsley
- 4 to 5 cloves garlic, crushed
- 1 tsp. sea salt
- 2 tsp. dried tarragon
- ¾ tsp. minced fresh basil

Instructions:

- Step 1: Combine the dried spices in the spice grinder and grind to make a fine powder. You can also grind these spices with a mortar and pestle, or mini food processor.
- Step 2: Add the spices to the liquids, then add to the ground pork.
- Step 3: Mix to incorporate the spices into the meat completely.
- Step 4: Cover with plastic wrap and refrigerate overnight.
- Step 5: Preheat the air fryer to 176 C.
- Step 6: Form 125g to 225g patties gently with your hands. Place on a rimmed cookie sheet, spacing about a 2.5-cm apart. You may need two cookie sheets, depending on how thick you make the patties.
- Step 7: Bake the sausage patties for about 15 to 25 minutes and serve immediately.

06 CANDIED WALNUTS

- This one's a deliciously sweet but slightly salty snack to start your day. Prepared with walnuts, cinnamon, and other ingredients, it's a perfect dish to add protein to your meals.
- **Preparation Time:** 5 minutes
- **Cooking Time: 10** minutes

Servings: 4

Per serving:

Kcal: 210; Fat: 10; Carbs: 18g; Protein: 10g; Sugars: 6g; Fibre: 3g

Ingredients:

- 4 tbsp. unsalted butter melted
- 100g walnuts, halved
- 2 tsp. vanilla extract
- 1 tbsp. sugar
- 3 tbsp. brown sugar
- ½ tsp. salt
- ½ tsp. cinnamon

Instructions:

- Step 1: Preheat the air fryer to 176 C. Place the walnuts in a bowl and add melted butter and vanilla.
- Step 2: Stir the walnuts to ensure they are well coated with butter and vanilla so that the other ingredients can stick to them.
- Step 3: Stir in the sugar, brown sugar, cinnamon, and salt, and toss the walnuts so that they are evenly covered.
- Step 4: Transfer them to the air fryer basket and cook for 10 minutes, shaking the basket halfway through.

07 COURGETTE CHIPS

- Freshly cut courgette dipped in breadcrumbs can be cooked in your air fryer to perfection, making a delicious addition to your other healthy air fryer dishes for breakfast.
- **Preparation Time:** 10 minutes
- **Cooking Time:** 8 minutes

Servings: 4
Per serving:

Kcal: 110; Fat: 10; Carbs: 6g; Protein: 4g; Sugars: 2g; Fibre: 2g

Ingredients:

- 2 courgettes
- 50g breadcrumbs
- ½ tsp. garlic powder
- ¼ tsp. onion powder
- 1 egg
- 3 tsp. flour

Instructions:

- Step 1: Cut courgettes to make thin slices, about ½-cm in thickness.
- Step 2: Mix breadcrumbs, onion powder, and garlic powder in a bowl.
- Step 3: Put the flour in another bowl. Whisk one egg in the third bowl. Dip the courgette into the flour, then into the egg, and lastly, into the breadcrumbs.
- Step 4: Place the coated courgette in a single layer in your air fryer and cook for 7 to 9 minutes at 180 C, flipping halfway through the cooking time.

08 ROASTED BROCCOLI

- The rich flavors and fragrance of roasted broccoli will soothe your senses and add a bunch of nutrients, including several minerals and vitamins to your meals.
- **Preparation Time:** 5 minutes
- **Cooking Time: 15** minutes

Servings: 4

Per serving:

Kcal: 240; Fat: 18g; Carbs: 38g; Protein: 18g; Sugars: 8g; Fibre: 7g

Ingredients:

- 200g broccoli florets
- 6 to 8 cloves garlic, minced
- 1 tsp. finely grated lemon zest
- 1 tbsp. avocado oil or olive oil
- ¼ tsp. sea salt or truffle salt
- 1 bunch fresh parsley, chopped
- 1 tsp. fresh yoghurt

Instructions:

- Step 1: Preheat the air fryer to 176 C.
- Step 2: Toss the broccoli florets and stems in a casserole dish, and add avocado oil, lemon zest, garlic, yoghurt, and salt.
- Step 3: Roast for about 25 to 35 minutes or until the broccoli florets and stems are fully cooked.
- Step 4: Stir once halfway through the cooking. Remove the dish from the oven and garnish with fresh parsley. Serve warm.

09 BROILED PORK CHOPS

- Broiled Pork Chops will nourish your body with their rich content of proteins and healthy fats.
- Preparation Time: 5 minutes
- Cooking Time: 15 minutes

Servings: 4

Per serving:

Kcal: 170; Fat: 13g; Carbs: 24g; Protein: 12g; Sugars: 7g; Fibre: 7g

Ingredients:

- 4 2-cm thick pork chops
- 2 tsp. marjoram leaves, dried
- 2 tsp. dried savory
- 1 tsp. dried oregano leaves
- 3 tsp. dried thyme leaves
- 1 tsp. dried tarragon
- ½ tsp. dried rubbed sage
- 1 tsp. dried rosemary leaves
- 2 tsp. yoghurt

Instructions:

- Step 1: Mix 1 to 2 tablespoons of the herbs of your choice and yoghurt, then sprinkle the seasoning over both the sides of pork chops liberally.
- Step 2: Allow the air fryer to preheat to 176 C for about 10 minutes.
- Step 3: Place the pork chops on the shelf of the air fryer and allow to cook for 6 to 8 minutes
- Step 4: Flip and broil the second side for another 6 to 8 minutes. Remove and serve immediately.

10 BANANA BREAD

- This true family classic been passed down to us for several generations and yet never loses its relevance. The only difference now is that we can prepare it using an air fryer, making it a much healthier option.
- **Preparation Time:** 10 minutes
- **Cooking Time:** 20 minutes

Servings: 4

Per serving:

Kcal: 290; Fat: 20g; Carbs: 33g; Protein: 18g; Sugars: 10g; Fibre: 12G

Ingredients:

- 100g flour
- 3 overripe bananas
- 25ml milk
- 1 tsp. of baking soda
- 1 tsp. of baking powder
- 1 tsp. of cinnamon
- 5 to 6 tsp. sugar
- 1 tsp. of salt
- 1 tsp. oil

Instructions:

- Step 1: Mix all of the ingredients in a large mixing bowl and transfer the contents to the air fryer basket.
- Step 2: Cook in the air fryer at 176 C for 20 to 30 minutes.
- Step 3: Allow to cool, then cut into thin slices. Serve immediately.

11 APPLE FRITTERS

- Making apple fritters in an air fryer allows you to skip the mess of deep frying. These fritters are prepared with a fast-leavened batter that does not use yeast. You just have to mix the batter and start cooking right away.
- Preparation Time: 10 minutes
- Cooking Time: 20 minutes

Servings: 4

Per serving:

Kcal: 220; Fat: 29g; Carbs: 48g; Protein: 19g; Sugars: 12g; Fibre: 12g

Ingredients:

- 2 large apples
- 150g all-purpose flour
- 1 tsp. baking powder
- 2 eggs
- 1 tsp. cinnamon
- 8 tbsp. granulated sugar
- ½ tsp. ground nutmeg
- 1 tsp. salt
- ¼ tsp. ground cloves
- 4 tbsp. apple cider or apple juice
- 1 tsp. vanilla
- 3 tsp. butter, melted
- Apple Cider Glaze:
- 8 tbsp. powdered sugar
- 10ml apple juice
- ¼ tsp. nutmeg
- ½ tsp. cinnamon

Instructions:

- Step 1: Peel and core the apples. Chop them into small pieces. Spread the pieces out on a clean kitchen towel and pat dry the moisture off.
- Step 2: Combine the sugar, flour, baking powder, spices, and salt in a bowl. Mix the apples into the flour.
- Step 3: Whisk the apple cider, melted butter, eggs, and vanilla in a small bowl. Mix the flour mixture and the wet mixture.
- Step 4: Preheat the air fryer to 176 C. Scoop 3 to 4 dollops of fritter dough using an ice cream scooper and place into the air fryer.
- Step 5: Spray the top of each fritter with oil. Cook for 5 to 6 minutes.
- Step 6: Flip over and cook for another 4 to 5 minutes.
- Step 7: Gently whisk the apple cider, powdered sugar, and spices. Drizzle the glaze over the fritters. Allow to sit for 8 to 10 minutes until the glaze sets well, then serve.

12 BROILED ASPARAGUS

- Broiled asparagus is a great way to add loads of fibre to your diet. This will nourish your gut flora and improve your bowel movements.
- **Preparation Time:** 5 minutes
- **Cooking Time:** 6 minutes

Servings: 4

Per serving:

Kcal: 120; Fat: 10g; Carbs: 14g; Protein: 9g; Sugars: 4g; Fibre: 4g

Ingredients:

- ½kg asparagus, tough ends of the spears snapped and discarded
- ¼ tsp, sea salt or truffle salt
- 2 tsp. avocado oil
- 1 tsp. cream

Instructions:

- Step 1: Place the asparagus on the shelves of your air fryer. Add cream and mix well. Sprinkle oil and salt and toss to combine.
- Step 2: Set the air fryer to 176 C and cook for 5 to 8 minutes.
- Step 3: Remove and serve immediately.

13   AIR FRYER PIZZA

- This is a good recipe to try when you are looking for something simple yet tasty for breakfast. This is such an easy throw-together pizza that it will win your family over.
- Preparation Time: 5 minutes
- Cooking Time: 15 minutes

Servings: 4

Per serving:

Kcal: 198; Fat: 32g; Carbs: 44g; Protein: 18g; Sugars: 10g; Fibre: 9g

Ingredients:

- Crescent Dough
- Crumbled sausage
- 3 scrambled eggs
- ½ chopped pepper
- 8 tbsp. mozzarella cheese
- 8 tbsp. cheddar cheese

Instructions:

Step 1: Gently spread the dough in the bottom of a springform pan and place it in the air fryer.
Cook at 176 C for 5 minutes or until the top of the dough is slightly brown
Step 2: Remove from the air fryer. Top with sausage, peppers, eggs, and cheese.
Step 3: Place in again the air fryer for an additional 5 to 10 minutes. Remove and serve.

14 BLUEBERRY MUFFINS

- Blueberry muffins offer an easy and quick way to save time for breakfast preparation. It will give you an energy boost in the morning hours and allow you to get going with your day feeling fresh.
- **Preparation Time:** 10 minutes
- **Cooking Time:** 15 minutes

Servings: 4

Per serving:

Kcal: 260; Fat: 29g; Carbs: 39g; Protein: 18g; Sugars: 18g; Fibre: 8g

Ingredients:

- 100g all-purpose or whole wheat flour
- 50g blueberries
- 50g old-fashioned oats (oatmeal)
- 5 tbsp. brown sweetener
- 50ml milk
- 1 tsp. cinnamon
- 1 tsp. baking powder
- ½ tsp. salt
- 4 tsp. melted unsalted butter
- 2 eggs
- 2 tsp. vanilla

Instructions:

Step 1: Combine the rolled oats, flour, salt, brown sweetener, cinnamon, and baking powder in a large mixing bowl and mix well.

Step 2: Combine the eggs, vanilla, milk, and butter in a separate bowl.

Step 3: Then, add the wet ingredients to the dry ingredients and stir. Add in the blueberries and mix well gently.

Step 4: Divide this batter among 12 muffin cups and place them on the shelf of the air fryer.

Step 5: Place the air fryer at 176 C and cook for 11 to 15 minutes checking once or twice in between. Remove and serve.

15 FRENCH TOAST STICKS

- These thick slices of bread, air-fried to perfection, are great to have when you are looking for a special breakfast without all the fuss.
- Preparation Time: 5 minutes
- Cooking Time: 32 minutes

Servings: 4

Per serving:

Kcal: 323; Fat: 50g; Carbs: 48g; Protein: 29g; Sugars: 20g; Fibre: 18g

Ingredients:

- 6 slices thick white bread
- 4 large eggs
- 25g granulated sugar
- 2 tbsp. milk
- 1 tsp. ground cinnamon
- ½ tsp. vanilla extract

Instructions:

Step 1: Spray the air fryer basket generously with cooking spray. Allow it to preheat for about 5 minutes at 176 C.

Step 2: Slice each piece of bread into 4 sticks by cutting them in halves vertically, and then, horizontally.

Step 3: Combine eggs, vanilla extract, milk, and half a portion of cinnamon in a medium size bowl. Whisk together until the ingredients are well blended.

Step 4: In another bowl, combine sugar and the remaining portion of cinnamon to prepare the cinnamon-sugar mixture.

Step 5: Dunk each breadstick into the egg mixture, soaking for about 5 seconds on each side. Make sure each slice is coated on both sides.

Step 6: Sprinkle cinnamon sugar mixture on each side and place the sticks in the fryer.

Step 7: Cook for 4 minutes, and flip. Then, cook for another 4 minutes. Serve with maple syrup or whipped cream.

15 FRENCH TOAST STICKS

These thick slices of bread, air-fried to perfection, are great to have when you are looking for a special breakfast without all the fuss.

Preparation Time: 5 minutes

Cooking Time: 32 minutes

Servings: 4

Per serving:

Kcal: 323; Fat: 50g; Carbs: 48g; Protein: 29g; Sugars: 20g; Fibre: 18g

Ingredients:

- 6 slices thick white bread
- 4 large eggs
- 25g granulated sugar
- 2 tbsp. milk
- 1 tsp. ground cinnamon
- ½ tsp. vanilla extract

Instructions:

Step 1: Spray the air fryer basket generously with cooking spray. Allow it to preheat for about 5 minutes at 176 C.

Step 2: Slice each piece of bread into 4 sticks by cutting them in halves vertically, and then, horizontally.

Step 3: Combine eggs, vanilla extract, milk, and half a portion of cinnamon in a medium size bowl. Whisk together until the ingredients are well blended.

Step 4: In another bowl, combine sugar and the remaining portion of cinnamon to prepare the cinnamon-sugar mixture.

Step 5: Dunk each breadstick into the egg mixture, soaking for about 5 seconds on each side. Make sure each slice is coated on both sides.

Step 6: Sprinkle cinnamon sugar mixture on each side and place the sticks in the fryer.

Step 7: Cook for 4 minutes, and flip. Then, cook for another 4 minutes. Serve with maple syrup or whipped cream.

16   SWEET POTATO HASH

- Sweet potato hash is stunningly good for breakfast. It is loaded with the goodness of proteins and complex carbohydrates that can add a punch of energy while performing important tasks during your day ahead.
- **Preparation Time:** 15 minutes
- **Cooking Time:** 20 minutes

Servings: 4

Per serving:

Kcal: 200; Fat: 37g; Carbs: 39g; Protein: 18g; Sugars: 14g; Fibre: 10g

Ingredients:

- 4 strips of bacon, diced
- 2 sweet potatoes, cut into small cubes
- 2 yellow onions, diced
- 2 tsp. dark brown sugar
- 2 tsp. olive oil
- 1 tsp. fresh rosemary, chopped
- ½ tsp. kosher salt
- ½ tsp. coarse ground black pepper

Instructions:

Step 1: Preheat the air fryer to 176 C. Sprinkle diced bacon with brown sugar in a small bowl. Mix to coat well and set aside.

Step 2: In another bowl, add diced sweet potatoes, and combine rosemary, olive oil, salt, and pepper. Stir well until potatoes are thoroughly coated.

Step 3: Add the mixture to the air fryer basket and cook for 8 to 10 minutes.

Step 4: Open the air fryer basket and stir the mixture. Add brown sugar-coated bacon to the hash and return to the air fryer.

Step 5: Cook for 10 minutes. Remove and serve.

17 HASH BROWN PATTIES

- Preparing hash brown patties in the air fryer saves you plenty of time. This dish is perfect to try when you are craving for your favourite patties but don't have enough time to prepare it the traditional way.
- **Preparation Time:** 0 minutes
- **Cooking Time:** 20 minutes

Servings: 4

Per serving:

Kcal: 270; Fat: 39g; Carbs: 44g; Protein: 21g; Sugars: 13g; Fibre: 10g

Ingredients:

- 4 frozen hash brown patties
- 2 tsp. black pepper, optional to taste
- 1 tsp. salt, optional to taste

Instructions:

Step 1: Place the frozen hash brown patties in the basket of your air fryer. Spread the patties in an even layer.

Step 2: Air Fry at 176 C for 10 minutes.

Step 3: Flip the patties over. Continue to cook for an additional 2 to 5 minutes or until they are crisped to your liking.

Step 4: Season with salt and pepper and serve.

18 ALMOND CANDIES

- Almond candies can be prepared in advance and stored. You can eat them for your breakfast as your mid-meal snacks or as a side dish for your lunch and dinner.
- **Preparation Time:** 5 minutes
- **Cooking Time:** 10 minutes

Servings: 4

Per serving:

Kcal: 240; Fat: 16; Carbs: 24g; Protein: 14g; Sugars: 8g; Fibre: 6g

Ingredients:

- 4 tbsp. unsalted butter melted
- 100g almonds, halved
- 2 tsp. vanilla extract
- 1 tbsp. sugar
- 3 tbsp. brown sugar
- ½ tsp. salt
- ½ tsp. cinnamon.

Instructions:

Step 1: Preheat the air fryer to 176 C. Place the almonds in a bowl and add melted butter and vanilla.

Step 2: Stir the almonds to ensure they are well coated with butter and vanilla so that the other ingredients can stick to them.

Step 3: Stir in the sugar, brown sugar, cinnamon, and salt, and toss the almonds so that they are evenly covered.

Step 4: Transfer them to the air fryer basket and cook for 10 minutes, shaking the basket halfway through.

19 CINNAMON ROLLS

- Cinnamon rolls are perfect for breakfast on any day, especially when you want to start your morning with a mix of different flavours.
- **Preparation Time:** 10 minutes
- **Cooking Time:** 20 minutes

Servings: 4

Per serving:

Kcal: 180; Fat: 18g; Carbs: 24g; Protein: 8g; Sugars: 8g; Fibre: 7g

Ingredients:

- 100g cinnamon rolls
- 1 tsp. cream or yoghurt
- 1 tsp. rosemary
- 1 tsp. thyme
- 1 tsp. powdered sugar (optional)

Instructions:

Step 1: Mix all the ingredients well and ensure the cinnamon rolls are well coated with the ingredients.

Step 2: Place the cinnamon rolls in the basket of the air fryer, and spray non-stick cooking oil.

Step 3: Cook at 176 C for 12 minutes, turning once. Remove and serve.

20 CREAMY BASIL WITH SPAGHATTI SQUASH

Creamy Basil Pesto Sauce is easy to make. You can prepare it in bulk and use it for preparing any dish to add some zest to it.

Preparation Time: 30 minutes

Cooking Time: 30 minutes

Servings: 4

Per serving:

Kcal: 340; Fat: 38g; Carbs: 48g; Protein: 29g; Sugars: 20g; Fibre: 17g

Ingredients:

Creamy Basil Pesto Sauce:

- 2 bunches fresh basil, chopped
- 2 garlic cloves
- 1 tbsp. extra-virgin olive oil
- Pinch of ground black pepper
- Pinch of sea salt
- 50ml water

Spaghetti Squash:

- 1 spaghetti squash, seeds discarded
- 1 tsp. coconut oil
- 1 head cauliflower
- 1 carrot, finely chopped
- 1 courgette, grated
- 1 bunch fresh spinach.

Instructions:

Step 1: Prepare Creamy Basil Pesto Sauce by blending together all the ingredients in a high-speed blender until a smooth mixture is formed. You can store the sauce in the refrigerator for 7 to 10 days.

Step 2: To prepare Spaghetti Squash, preheat the air fryer to 176 C.

Step 3: Then, grease a baking sheet. Cut the squash into halves and place each half face-down on to the sheet.

Step 4: Bake them for 20 to 30 minutes, or until they are soft.

Step 5: Remove the sheet from the oven. Turn the squash face-up using hot pads or tongs. Allow to cool for 10 minutes.

Step 6: While squash is cooking, sauté the carrot chunks and cauliflower florets in a medium saucepan until cooked through

Step 7: When the squash is done, heat coconut oil in a pan set over low heat. Scoop out the flesh of spaghetti squash using a spoon and add it to the pan along with the spinach, courgette, and Creamy Basil Pesto Sauce.

Step 8: Stir well to combine and heat the mixture for about 5 minutes. Mix in the carrot and cauliflower florets and serve.

21 ROASTED SALMON WITH TANGY MANGO SALSA

Seafood like salmon provides a good source of healthy fats like omega-3 fatty acids that can protect you against the risk of high cholesterol, heart disease, and chronic inflammation. Mango salsa is the perfect side dish for your main course at lunch as well as dinner. This combination will satisfy your craving for a delicious and filling meal

Ingredients:

- Brown mustard, preferably made with apple cider vinegar
- 2 large wild-caught salmon fillets
- 1 tsp. extra-virgin olive oil
- Ground black pepper to taste
- Salt to taste
- 6 tsp. mango Salsa

Salmon Sauce:

- 1½ tsp. chopped fresh parsley
- 2 tsp. extra-virgin olive oil
- 3 tsp. prepared brown mustard
- 2 tsp. chopped fresh dill
- 1 to 2 tsp. fresh lemon juice
- 1 garlic clove, minced

Tangy Mango Salsa:

- 1 mango, chopped
- 1 avocado, chopped
- ½ red onion, chopped
- 3 tsp. chopped fresh cilantro
- 3 tsp. lemon zest
- 1 tsp. olive oil
- Juice of 1 small lemon
- Pinch of salt

Instructions:

Step 1: To prepare Tangy Mango Salsa, stir together all the ingredients in a large bowl, until they are well combined and sprinkle salt.

Step 2: Preheat the oven to 176 C.

Step 3: Coat each side of both the salmon fillets with olive oil and sprinkle salt and pepper.

Step 4: Place the fillets on a rimmed baking sheet in the bottom rack of an oven. Roast it for about 20 minutes, or until it is heated and has become flaky.

Step 5: Combine all the ingredients for the salmon sauce in a bowl and pour it over the fillets before serving.

Step 6: Top each fillet with the Tangy Mango Salsa..

22 CREAMY ACORN SQUASH

- This delicious squash will just melt in your mouth thanks to the sweet spices and coconut oil added to it!
- **Preparation Time:** 5 minutes
- **Cooking Time: 40** minutes

Servings: 4

Per serving:

Kcal: 340; Fat: 30g; Carbs: 28g; Protein: 20g; Sugars: 8g; Fibre: 8g

Ingredients:

- 1 acorn squash
- 2 tsp. coconut oil
- Little coconut oil for greasing the baking dish
- Pinch of ground cinnamon
- Pinch of ground nutmeg

Instructions:

Step 1: Preheat the air fryer to 176 C.

Step 2: Cut the squash in 2 halves from top to bottom.

Step 3: Remove the seeds gently using a spoon and discard them.

Step 4: Grease a baking dish with coconut oil. Place the squash halves face-down onto the baking dish and bake them for about 30 minutes. Turn each squash half face-up using tongs.

Step 5: Add 1 teaspoon of the coconut oil over each half and sprinkle the cinnamon and nutmeg. Cook for another 5 minutes before serving.

23 SPICY FISH TACO

- The crunchy texture of tacos will be great for your taste buds. Each bite of these crunchy tacos will help you forget your stress and feel better.
- Preparation Time: 10 minutes
- Cooking Time: 25 minute

Servings: 4

Per serving:

Kcal: 366; Fat: 25g; Carbs: 21g; Protein: 12g; Sugars: 12g; Fibre: 10g

Ingredients:

- 3 wild-caught whitefish fillets
- Juice of 2 limes
- 1 tsp. ground black pepper
- 1 tsp. sea salt
- 1 garlic clove, minced
- 1 to 2 tsp. extra-virgin olive oil
- 8 lettuce or cabbage leaves
- ¼ tsp. ground turmeric
- ½ red onion, minced
- ½ head red cabbage, cored and thinly sliced
- A bunch fresh cilantro, chopped
- 2 avocados, sliced
- 1 large lime, cut into wedges, as a garnish

Instructions:

Step 1: Preheat the air fryer to 176 C.

Step 2: Place the whitefish fillets in a basket of the air fryer. Sprinkle each with salt and pepper. Drizzle the olive oil and lime juice, coating both the sides.

Step 3: Top each fillet with turmeric and garlic. Bake the fish for about 25 minutes, or until the fillets are flaky.

Step 4: Place the cabbage leaves or lettuce on 4 serving plates and top them with the flaked fish, along with the sliced cabbage, avocado, onion, and cilantro.

Step 5: Drizzle each plate with lime juice and garnish with a lime wedge

24 BRUSSELS SPROUTS WITH CHERRIES

- Brussels sprouts contain proteins that support the body's repair mechanisms while the cherries will boost your immunity by providing vitamin C and other nutrients.
- Preparation Time: 5 minutes
- Cooking Time: 15 minutes

Servings: 4

Per serving:

Kcal: 210; Fat: 15g; Carbs: 18g; Protein: 15g; Sugars: 10g; Fibre: 10g

Ingredients:

- 200g organic Brussels sprouts, with stems chopped off
- 2 to 3 tsp. olive oil or coconut oil, melted
- ¼ tsp. salt
- 100g fresh organic cherries.

Instructions:

Step 1: Preheat the air fryer to 176 C.

Step 2: Place the whitefish fillets in a basket of the air fryer. Sprinkle each with salt and pepper. Drizzle the olive oil and lime juice, coating both the sides.

Step 3: Top each fillet with turmeric and garlic. Bake the fish for about 25 minutes, or until the fillets are flaky.

Step 4: Place the cabbage leaves or lettuce on 4 serving plates and top them with the flaked fish, along with the sliced cabbage, avocado, onion, and cilantro.

Step 5: Drizzle each plate with lime juice and garnish with a lime wedge

25 AIR FRYER SAUSAGE PATTIES

- Sausage patties can be a delicious side dish to any lunch menu. You can cook them fresh as well as frozen!
- Preparation Time: 6 minutes
- Cooking Time: 6 minutes

Servings: 4

Per serving:

Kcal: 166; Fat: 35g; Carbs: 28g; Protein: 15g; Sugars: 13g; Fibre: 10g

Ingredients:

- 8 raw sausage patties.

Instructions:

Step 1: Preheat your air fryer to 176 C.

Step 2: Place the sausage patties in the air fryer in one single layer without overlapping.

Step 3: Cook for 6 to 8 minutes. Remove from the fryer and enjoy

26 CHURROS

- Churros can be fried in your air fryer to golden perfection. It is a delicious dessert to have to start your day feeling fresh and energetic.
- Preparation Time: 10 minutes
- Cooking Time: 10 minutes

Servings: 4

Per serving:

Kcal: 204; Fat: 25g; Carbs: 27g; Protein: 6g; Sugars: 15g; Fibre: 10g

Ingredients:

- 100ml water
- 2 tbsp. granulated sugar
- 8 tsp. unsalted butter,
- 2 large eggs
- 100g all-purpose flour
- 1 tsp. vanilla extract
- ¼ tsp. salt
- Oil spray
- 8 tbsp. granulated sugar
- ¾ tsp. ground cinnamon

Instructions:

Step 1: Put a baking mat on a baking sheet. Spray it with very little oil spray.

Step 2: In a saucepan add water, sugar, butter, and salt and bring to a boil over medium heat.

Step 3: Reduce the heat to low and add flour. Stir constantly with a spatula until the dough comes together and becomes smooth. Remove from heat. Transfer the dough to a medium bowl. Let it cool for 4 minutes.

Step 4: Add vanilla extract and eggs to the bowl and blend well using an electric hand mixer until the dough comes together. The mixture should look like gluey or mashed potatoes.

Step 5: Press the lumps together into a ball using your hands and transfer them to a piping bag fitted with a star-shaped tip.

Step 6: Pipe the churros onto the baking mat, in 10-cm lengths. Cut the end with scissors. Refrigerate the piped churros on the baking sheet for about one hour.

Step 7: Transfer the churros to the air fryer basket carefully using a cookie spatula, leaving about 2-cm space between two churros. Spray the churros with oil spray.

Step 8: Air fry at 176 C for 10 to 12 minutes or until golden brown.to the bowl of sugar mixture immediately and toss to coat. Serve warm with chocolate dipping sauce.

Step 9: Combine granulated sugar and cinnamon in a shallow bowl. Transfer the baked churros

27 EGG ROLLS

- These egg rolls are a fun and delicious addition to your breakfast. These are stuffed with cheese and bacon giving you loads of protein. These egg rolls are also easy to make and can be prepared ahead of time.
- Preparation Time: 10 minutes
- Cooking Time: 10 minutes

Servings: 4

Per serving:

Kcal: 258; Fat: 10g; Carbs: 10g; Protein: 12g; Sugars: 4g; Fibre: 4g

Ingredients:

- 4 tortilla wraps
- 4 slices bacon, cooked and crumbled
- 10 tbsp. cheese, shredded
- 4 eggs
- 1 tsp. salt
- 1 tsp. pepper
- 1 tsp. butter.

Instructions:

- Step 1: Preheat the air fryer to 376 C.
- Step 2: Crack the eggs in a small bowl, and season with salt and pepper. Whisk until well blended.
- Step 3: Add butter to a frying pan, over low heat.
- Step 4: Sprinkle the crumbled bacon and cheese onto the eggs and stir well to combine until the eggs are thoroughly cooked.
- Step 5: Place a tortilla wrap on a flat surface. Brush the edges of the tortilla wrap with water.
- Step 6: Place a small quantity of the egg mixture onto the centre of the tortilla wrap. Fold in the corners, and then fold the bottom corner up. Then, roll the tortilla wrap away from you and seal the top with some more water. Repeat the same with each tortilla wrap.
- Step 7: Place the tortilla wraps in the air fryer basket such that they are not touching or
- overlapping. Lightly brush with canola or olive oil.
- Step 8: Air fry for 8 to 10 minutes, flipping halfway through at about 5 minutes..

28 QUICK AND SIMPLE TOAST

- If you are in a hurry or are just tired, you can always rely on this simple and quick toast recipe to fill your tummy. With an air fryer, your toast will be ready to eat within just a few minutes.
- Preparation Time: 10 minutes
- Cooking Time: 4 minute

Servings: 4

Per serving:

Kcal: 160; Fat: 14g; Carbs: 12g; Protein: 10g; Sugars: 4g; Fibre: 4g

Ingredients:

- 2 slices of bread
- 2 tsp. peanut butter or unsalted butter.

Instructions:

- Step 1: Add the slices of bread to the air fryer basket and set the temperature to 204 C.
- Step 2: Air fry for 3 to 4 minutes. If the slices of bread are very thin, your toast will be done in just 2 to 3 minutes. If you like your toast more brown or dark, add 30 seconds more.
- Step 3: Spread peanut butter, jelly, avocado, or any other topping or spread of your choice and serve.

29 SPICY SALTED WALNUTS

- This one's a tempting salty snack that also goes as a side dish for your breakfast menu. Prepared with walnuts and other ingredients, this dish packs in loads of protein to your diet.
- Preparation Time: 5 minutes
- Cooking Time: 10 minutes

Servings: 4

Per serving:

Kcal: 98; Fat: 7; Carbs: 10g; Protein: 8g; Sugars: 4g; Fibre: 3g

Ingredients:

- 100g walnuts, halved
- 4 tbsp. unsalted butter melted
- 1 tsp. salt
- 1 tsp. pepper
- 1 tsp. ginger powder
- 1 tsp. garlic powder
- 1 tsp. cumin powder
- 1 tsp. coriander powder
- ½ tsp. cinnamon.

Instructions:

- Step 1: Preheat the air fryer to 176 C. Place the walnuts in a bowl and add melted butter.
- Step 2: Stir the walnuts to ensure they are well coated with butter so that the other ingredients can stick to them.
- Step 3: Stir in the remaining spices and toss the walnuts so that they are evenly covered.
- Step 4: Transfer them to the air fryer basket and cook for 10 minutes, shaking the basket halfway through.

30 FRIED EGGS

- This is another quick recipe you can try when you are not in the mood to make an elaborate breakfast. It provides a good source of protein and calcium. You will enjoy the creamy yolk and crispy edges without all the guilt of eating fried eggs prepared in traditional methods.
- Preparation Time: 3 minutes
- Cooking Time: 3 minutes

Servings: 4

Per serving:

Kcal: 198; Fat: 36g; Carbs: 45g; Protein: 10g; Sugars: 12g; Fibre: 10g

Ingredients:

- 4 large eggs
- 1 tsp. salt
- ½ tsp. black pepper

Instructions:

- Step 1: Spray your air fryer pan with little olive oil, just enough to coat the pan. Crack the eggs into the pan.
- Step 2: Set the temperature of your air fryer to 176 C. Place the pan into the fryer and cook for 3 minutes.
- Step 3: Remover carefully, sprinkle salt and pepper, and serve immediately.

Please scan the QR code below to access your bonus PDF with all 150 recipes with full coloured photos & beautiful designs alongside! This is the only way we can get the recipes with coloured photos to you & keep the book as reasonably priced as possible.

Also, once downloaded you can take the PDF with you digitally wherever you go- meaning you can cook these recipes wherever you may be! (As long as you have an air fryer!)

We hope you enjoy and do let us know your feedback!

STEP BY STEP Guide To Access-

1. Open Your Phones (Or Any Device You Want The Book On) Back Camera. The Back Camera Is The One You use as if you are taking a picture of someone.
2. Simply point your Camera at the QR code and 'tap' the QR code with your finger to focus the camera.
3. A link / pop up will appear. Simply tap that (and make sure you have internet connection) and the
4. FREE PDF containing all of the coloured images should appear.
5. Now you have access to these FOREVER. Simply 'Bookmark' The tab it opened on, or download the document and take wherever you want.
6. Repeat this on any device you want it on! (If you want it on a laptop, simply email the document to yourself!)
7. Any issues please email us at *vicandersonpublishing@gmail.com* and we will be happy to help!!

03

SECTION 3

LUNCH RECIPES

01 FROZEN WAFFLES

- Frozen waffles are very tempting and pleasing for your taste buds. You can enjoy them after your lunch or dinner or serve the dish to your guests to impress them with your cooking skills.
- Preparation Time: 6 minutes
- Cooking Time: 36 minutes

Servings: 4

Per serving:

Kcal: 200; Fat: 25g; Carbs: 27g; Protein: 10g; Sugars: 16g; Fibre: 8g

Ingredients:

- 4 frozen waffles.

Instructions:

- Step 1: Place the frozen waffles in the basket of the air fryer and spread each in an even layer making sure they do not overlap.
- Step 2: Air fry at 180 C for 4 to 5 minutes.
- Step 3: Flip over the waffles and continue to air fry for another 2 minutes or until they are done to your preferred doneness..

02 CHEESE AND HONEY SCRAMBLED EGGS

- Cheese and honey scrambled eggs offer the perfect way to satisfy your early morning hunger pangs while getting a good amount of proteins and many other nutrients.
- Preparation Time: 6 minutes
- Cooking Time: 36 minutes

Servings: 4

Per serving:

Kcal: 220; Fat: 29g; Carbs: 27g; Protein: 10g; Sugars: 16g; Fibre: 8g

Ingredients:

- 4 large eggs
- 2 tsp. butter
- 50ml milk
- 1 tsp. minced chives optional
- ½ tsp. salt
- ¼ tsp. black pepper

Instructions:

- Step 1: Add the butter to the aluminium tray. Place it into the bottom of your air fryer.
- Step 2: Set the air fryer temperature to 176 C.
- Step 3: Let the butter melt in the fryer and swirl the melted butter over the bottom of the tray.
- Step 4: In a bowl, whisk the eggs pepper, milk, salt, and chives. Pour the mixture into the tray in the air fryer.
- Step 5: Cook for 5 to 6 minutes, stopping to check midway through the time. Stir the eggs once or twice and remove them once they have done to your desired texture..

03 CRISPY CHICKEN CURRY DRUMSTICKS

- These chicken drumsticks are crispy and flavourful on the outside but juicy on the inside. You can spice them up by adding some red pepper flakes.
- Preparation Time: 35 minutes
- Cooking Time: 15 minutes

Servings: 4

Per serving:

Kcal: 190; Fat: 26g; Carbs: 28g; Protein: 10g; Sugars: 10g; Fibre: 8g

Ingredients:

- ½kg chicken drumsticks
- 3/4 tsp. salt, divided
- ½ tsp. onion salt
- 2 tsp. curry powder
- ½ tsp. garlic powder
- 2 tsp. olive oil
- Cilantro, chopped.

Instructions:

- Step 1: Place the chicken in a bowl and add ½ teaspoon salt and little water – just enough to cover it. Let it stand for 15 minutes and then drain. Pat dry gently.
- Step 2: Preheat the air fryer to 175 C. In another bowl, mix curry powder, oil, onion salt, garlic powder, and the remaining salt. Then, add chicken and toss well to coat evenly.
- Step 3: Place the chicken on the tray of the air-fryer basket in a single layer. Cook for 15 to 17 minutes, turning halfway through.
- Step 4: Sprinkle with cilantro and serve with avocado hash with bacon.

04 COCONUT SHRIMP

- Breadcrumbs and coconut flakes give this coconut shrimp recipe a great crunchy texture. It's perfect as an appetizer or as your main course.
- Preparation Time: 25 minutes
- Cooking Time: 10 minutes

Servings: 4

Per serving:

Kcal: 390; Fat: 40g; Carbs: 58g; Protein: 30g; Sugars: 20g; Fibre: 18g

Ingredients:

- 1kg uncooked shrimp
- 50g shredded coconut
- 25g breadcrumbs
- 4 large egg whites
- 3 tbsp. hot sauce
- ¼ tsp. salt
- ¼ tsp. pepper
- 50g all-purpose flour

Instructions:

- Step 1: Preheat the air fryer to 176 C. Peel and devein the shrimp, leaving the tails on.
- Step 2: In a small bowl, toss the coconut and breadcrumbs. In another bowl, combine the egg whites, salt and pepper, and add hot sauce. Place the flour in another bowl.
- Step 3: Dip the shrimps in the flour to coat them lightly and shake off the excess. Then, dip in the egg white mixture, and in the coconut mixture, patting gently to allow the coating to adhere.
- Step 4: Place the shrimp on a greased tray in the air-fryer basket in a single layer. Cook for 4 minutes. Turn the shrimp and cook for another 4 minutes until the coconut is lightly browned and the shrimp have turned pink.
- Step 5: Remove and serve with hot sauce.

05 SWEET AND SPICY MEATBALLS

- This recipe is great for those who love meatballs. It packs a sweet and savoury punch and keeps you feeling full for many hours.
- Preparation Time: 30 minutes
- Cooking Time: 10 minutes

Servings: 4

Per serving:

Kcal: 260; Fat: 30g; Carbs: 38g; Protein: 20g; Sugars: 10g; Fibre: 8g

Ingredients:

- 100g quick-cooking oats
- 1kg lean ground beef
- 50g crushed Ritz crackers
- 2 eggs, lightly beaten
- 100ml milk
- 1 tsp. garlic powder
- 1 tsp. dried minced onion
- 1 tsp. salt
- 1 tsp. ground cumin
- ½ tsp. pepper
- 1 tsp. honey

Instructions:

- Step 1: Preheat the air fryer to 180 C. In a bowl, combine all the ingredients except the beef, and mix well.
- Step 2: Then, add beef and mix gently. Shape the mixture into small meatballs.
- Step 3: Arrange the meatballs on a greased tray in the air-fryer basket in a single layer. Cook for 12 to 15 minutes or until they are lightly browned.
- Step 4: Serve with any sauce or dip of your choice.

06 CRISPY YAM

- Crispy yam, just as the name suggests, is crispy on the outside and soft on the inside. Yam is also a good source of fibre and complex carbs that can keep you feeling full and energetic for several hours without feeling hunger pangs.
- Preparation Time: 2 minutes
- Cooking Time: 15 minute

Servings: 4

Per serving:

Kcal: 120; Fat: 18g; Carbs: 28g; Protein: 10g; Sugars: 8g; Fibre: 8g

Ingredients:

- 4 large yams
- 1 tbsp. olive oil
- Seasoning of your choice
- ½ tsp. salt
- ½ tsp. black ground pepper
- ½ tsp. garlic powder.

Instructions:

- Step 1: Preheat the air fryer to 176 C for about 2 to 3 minutes.
- Step 2: Peel and cut the yam into small cubes.
- Step 3: Toss the yam with seasoning and oil, and make sure all the cubes are thoroughly coated.
- Step 4: Spray the basket of the air fryer with a non-stick spray and place the potatoes in it.
- Step 5: Cook for about 15 minutes. Stop and shake the basket 2 to 3 times throughout to ensure even cooking.
- Step 6: Transfer to a plate and serve immediately.

07 ROASTED ORANGES

- These roasted oranges with honey and cinnamon take just 5 minutes and make up for a perfectly delicious and savoury lunch menu.
- Preparation Time: 1 minutes
- Cooking Time: 3 minutes

Servings: 4

Per serving:

Kcal: 60; Fat: 8g; Carbs: 9g; Protein: 6g; Sugars: 3g; Fibre: 2g

Ingredients:

- 4 oranges
- 4 tsp. honey
- 2 tsp. cinnamon.

Instructions:

- Step 1: Remove the skin of the oranges and slice each orange in half.
- Step 2: Preheat an air fryer to 200 C.
- Step 3: Place the cut oranges in the air fryer and drizzle some honey and cinnamon on top.
- Step 4: Air fry the oranges for about 3 to 6 minutes or until they are golden on top. Serve immediately while they are still warm.

08 STRAWBERRY TURNOVER

- Strawberry turnover is rich in vitamin C, which boosts your immunity and acts as a powerful antioxidant. It will protect you against several immunological disorders and infections.
- Preparation Time: 10 minutes
- Cooking Time: 30 minutes

Servings: 4

Per serving:

Kcal: 180; Fat: 28g; Carbs: 30g; Protein: 16g; Sugars: 13g; Fibre: 12g

Ingredients:

- Kcal: 180; Fat: 28g; Carbs: 30g; Protein: 16g; Sugars: 13g; Fibre: 12g
- 25g sugar
- 1 Tsp. vanilla extract
- 2 pastry sheets.

Instructions:

- Step 1: Dissolve the cornstarch in water in a small bowl. Set it aside. In a saucepan, add the sugar, strawberries, and vanilla extract. Stir well and bring to a simmer for 12 to 15 minutes.
- Step 2: Remove the mixture from the heat and set aside to cool.
- Step 3: On a flat surface, roll out each puff pastry into a square and cut it into 4 even sizes.
- Step 4: Place 1 teaspoon of the strawberry mixture at the centre of the dough and roll over diagonally. Press down gently with your thumb, and again with a fork to seal it completely.
- Step 5: Place the pastries on the shelf of the air fryer and allow to cook for 18 minutes at 176 C.

09 BACON AND EGG CUPS

- This one's a low-carb, keto-friendly recipe suitable for calorie-conscious people trying to lose weight or maintain their blood sugar levels.
- Preparation Time: 5 minutes
- Cooking Time: 10 minutes

Servings: 4

Per serving:

Kcal: 160; Fat: 18g; Carbs: 20g; Protein: 10g; Sugars: 8g; Fibre: 7g

Ingredients:

- 4 eggs
- 4 pieces of bacon
- Salt and pepper to taste (optional)

Instructions:

- Step 1: Place the bacon in a muffin tin around its circular part, making a shallow basket with the bacon. Set it in the air fryer at 176 C for 5 minutes.
- Step 2: After 5 minutes, crack an egg into the centre of each circle of air-fried bacon. Set it back into the fryer for another 5 to 6 minutes.
- Step 3: Remove and serve immediately.

10 SAUSAGE CASSEROLE

- Sausage casserole is a fun-filled healthy recipe that is truly delicious. It is sure to help you continue with your hectic day with loads of energy.
- Preparation Time: 10 minutes
- Cooking Time: 20 minutees

Servings: 4

Per serving:

Kcal: 520; Fat: 58g; Carbs: 60g; Protein: 36g; Sugars: 33g; Fibre: 32g

Ingredients:

- ½kg hash browns
- 4 eggs
- ½kg ground sausage
- 1 green bell pepper, diced
- 1 yellow bell pepper diced
- 1 red bell pepper, diced
- 2 sweet onions, diced.

Instructions:

- Step 1: Foil line the air fryer basket and place the hash browns on the shelf. Top it with the sausage.
- Step 2: Place the peppers and onions evenly on top of the sausage.
- Step 3: Cook for 10 minutes at 176 C, stirring occasionally.
- Step 4: Remove carefully from the basket. Crack an egg into a bowl, and then pour it right on top of the casserole.
- Step 5: Cook for another 10 minutes. Sprinkle salt and pepper to taste and serve immediately

11   AVOCADO HASH WITH BACON

- Avocado with bacon is a stunningly good dish to have for your lunch as well as brunch. It can be prepared quickly.
- Preparation Time: 5 minutes
- Cooking Time: 20 minutes

Servings: 4

Per serving:

Kcal: 200; Fat: 37g; Carbs: 39g; Protein: 18g; Sugars: 14g; Fibre: 10g

Ingredients:

- 4 strips of bacon, diced
- 2 sweet potatoes, cut into small cubes
- 2 yellow onions, diced
- 2 tsp. dark brown sugar
- 2 tsp. olive oil
- 1 tsp. fresh rosemary, chopped
- ½ tsp. kosher salt
- ½ tsp. coarse ground black pepper.

Instructions:

- Step 1: Preheat the air fryer to 176 C. Sprinkle diced bacon with brown sugar in a small bowl. Mix to coat well and set aside.
- Step 2: In another bowl, add diced avocado, and combine rosemary, olive oil, salt, and pepper. Stir well until potatoes are thoroughly coated.
- Step 3: Add the mixture to the air fryer basket and cook for 8 to 10 minutes.
- Step 4: Open the air fryer basket and stir the mixture. Add brown sugar-coated bacon to the hash and return to the air fryer.
- Step 5: Cook for 10 minutes. Remove and serve.

12   CRISPY CHEESY COURGETTE FRITTERS

- This is a traditional sweet and fried doughnut recipe. After a makeover in the air fryer, this recipe has just become healthier and more savoury! The result is cheesy fritters cooked with minimal oil that goes great in your lunchboxes and also as a starter at your next party.
- Preparation Time: 10 minutes
- Cooking Time: 15 minutes

Servings: 4

Per serving:

Kcal: 280; Fat: 36g; Carbs: 38g; Protein: 18g; Sugars: 12g; Fibre: 8g

Ingredients:

- 500g courgette, coarsely grated
- 110g plain flour
- 55g coarsely grated mozzarella cheese
- 40g finely grated parmesan cheese
- 1 egg
- 2 tsp. sea salt flakes
- 2 garlic cloves, crushed
- 2 tbsp. basil pesto
- Tomato pasta sauce.

Instructions:

- Step 1: Place courgette in a colander and sprinkle salt. Set aside for 5 minutes. Squeeze out excess liquid. Transfer to a bowl. Add the flour, parmesan, mozzarella, pesto, garlic, and egg. Stir until well combined.
- Step 2: Line the air fryer basket with baking paper. Place 2 tablespoons of the mixture on the baking paper, keeping a little room between each serving.
- Step 3: Cook at 180 C for 15 minutes, turning the fritters halfway.
- Step 4: Serve with tomato pasta sauce for dipping.

13   BANANA MUFFINS

- Cooked in an air fryer, these easy banana muffins are moist and super fluffy. They make a great option for your lunchbox fillers.
- Preparation Time: 10 minutes
- Cooking Time: 10 minutes

Servings: 4

Per serving:

Kcal: 200; Fat: 37g; Carbs: 39g; Protein: 18g; Sugars: 14g; Fibre: 10g

Ingredients:

- 2 ripe bananas
- 60g brown sugar
- 150g all-purpose flour
- 1 egg
- 60ml buttermilk
- 60ml olive oil
- Maple syrup, to brush

Instructions:

- Step 1: Mash the bananas using a fork in a small bowl. Set aside for 5 minutes.
- Step 2: Whisk the flour and sugar in another bowl. Make a dip in the centre. Break up the egg with a whisk. Add the egg, buttermilk, and oil. Stir the mixture with a wooden spoon to combine well. Stir through the banana.
- Step 3: Preheat the air fryer to 180 C. Divide half of the mixture among 8 patty cases. Carefully transfer these cases to the rack of the air fryer and cook for 8 to 10 minutes or until the muffins are cooked through.
- Step 4: Brush the top of the muffins with maple syrup while still warm and serve immediately.

14 PIZZA BITES

- This recipe is so easy that even your kids can make it. In fact, your kids will love making these pizza bites. They are also perfect for popping in their lunch boxes.
- Preparation Time: 15 minutes
- Cooking Time: 15 minutes

Servings: 4

Per serving:

Kcal: 120; Fat: 24g; Carbs: 20g; Protein: 16g; Sugars: 8g; Fibre: 6g

Ingredients:

- 4 sheets of frozen puff pastry
- 70g pizza sauce
- 227g pineapple chunks, juice drained
- 80g shredded ham
- 70g shredded pizza cheese.

Instructions:

- Step 1: Preheat the air fryer to 200 C.
- Step 2: Grease the baking tray. Cut 6 discs from each pastry sheet using a round cutter.
- Step 3: Place them on the prepared tray and spread them evenly with pizza sauce. Top with pineapple, ham, and cheese.
- Step 4: Place the tray in the air fryer and bake for 15 minutes or until the cheese melts and the base is crisp. Serve immediately.

15 FETA NUGGETS

- These crispy and crusty bites of Feta nuggets can be served with a hot sauce and are perfect for your meat-free days.
- Preparation Time: 15 minutes
- Cooking Time: 6 minutes

Servings: 4

Per serving:

: Kcal: 280; Fat: 34g; Carbs: 36g; Protein: 26g; Sugars: 18g; Fibre: 16g

Ingredients:

- 1 tbsp. plain flour
- 1 tsp. dried chilli flakes
- 1 tsp. onion powder
- 1 egg
- 50g breadcrumbs
- 2 tsp. sesame seeds
- 180g Feta cheese, cut into 2-cm cubes
- Fresh chives, finely chopped.

Instructions:

- Step 1: Combine flour, chilli flakes, and onion powder in a bowl. Sprinkle with pepper.
- Step 2: Whisk the egg in another bowl. Combine sesame seeds and breadcrumbs in the bowl. Toss feta cheese in the flour mixture in batches. Dip in the egg, and then toss in the breadcrumb mixture to coat it well.
- Step 3: Preheat the air fryer to 180 C. Place the feta cubes on the shelf of the air fryer in a single layer. Cook for 6 minutes or until they become golden.
- Step 4: Remove from the air dryer and sprinkle with chives. Serve immediately with hot barbeque sauce.

16   LEMON CAKE

- This one's an easy-to-prepare lemon cake that you can cook in your air fryer in less than 30 minutes. You can serve it with a dollop of ice cream or just eat it as is.
- Preparation Time: 10 minutes
- Cooking Time: 25 minutes

Servings: 4

Per serving:

Kcal: 290; Fat: 36g; Carbs: 46g; Protein: 26g; Sugars: 28g; Fibre: 12g

Ingredients:

- 150g butter
- 140g caster sugar
- 225g all-purpose flour
- 2 eggs
- 2 tbsp. lemon rind, finely grated
- 50ml lemon juice.

Instructions:

- Step 1: Grease a round cake pan and line the base with a baking sheet.
- Step 2: Beat the butter, flour, sugar, eggs, and lemon juice and mix well using electric beaters for 3 to 4 minutes or until the mixture becomes pale and creamy. Spoon the batter into the pan.
- Step 3: Keep the pan in the basket of your air fryer. Set the air fryer to 160 C. Bake for 25 minutes or until a fork inserted in the centre comes out clean.
- Step 4: Serve the cake warm.

17 CHICKEN TENDERS

- These chicken tenders provide a good source of proteins. Served with garlic mayonnaise, this dish is sure to satisfy your craving for a sumptuous meal.
- Preparation Time: 10 minutes
- Cooking Time: 15 minut

Servings: 4

Per serving:

Kcal: 360; Fat: 46g; Carbs: 36g; Protein: 32g; Sugars: 18g; Fibre: 15g

Ingredients:

- 500g chicken tenderloins
- 5 tbsp. oregano or any other crumb seasoning of your choice
- Canola oil spray
- 8 to 10 tbsp. garlic mayonnaise
- 1 tbsp. grated ginger.

Instructions:

- Step 1: Place the chicken on a tray. Sprinkle with grated ginger and half of the seasoning and turn it. Sprinkle evenly with the remaining seasoning. Spray some oil.
- Step 2: Preheat the air fryer to 180 C. Place the chicken on the shelf of the fryer and cook for 15 minutes.
- Step 3: Remove and serve with garlic mayonnaise.

18   APPLE AND PORK SAUSAGE ROLLS

- hese easy sausage rolls can be your standalone dish for lunch. This one dish alone would be able to satisfy your hunger pangs and help you feel fuller for many hours to go.
- Preparation Time: 25 minutes
- Cooking Time: 35 minut

Servings: 4

Per serving:

Kcal: 320; Fat: 39g; Carbs: 36g; Protein: 28g; Sugars: 18g; Fibre: 10g

Ingredients:

- 500g pork mince
- 1 apple, peeled and grated
- 2 onions, chopped
- 8 tbsp. cheddar cheese, grated
- 2 garlic cloves, crushed
- 2 tbsp. parsley, chopped
- 2 eggs, lightly beaten
- 2 tsp. thyme leaves
- 4 sheets puff pastry
- 2 tsp. fennel seeds
- 2 tsp. sesame seeds
- Tomato sauce, to serve

Instructions:

- Step 1: Place the mince, apple, cheddar cheese, onion, garlic, thyme, parsley, and half the egg in a large bowl. Sprinkle salt and pepper and mix to combine well.
- Step 2: Place the sheets of pastry side by side on a clean flat surface. Cut each of them into halves to form 2 large rectangles. Leaving a 1-cm edge, add 2 tablespoons of the mince mixture along the long side of each pastry piece. Brush the edges with very little of the remaining egg. Roll up the pastry and close the filling. Trim the ends. Cut each roll into 3 or 4 pieces. Sprinkle with sesame seeds and fennel and season with salt and pepper.
- Step 3: Place the rolls, seam-side down, on the baking tray.
- Step 4: Preheat the air fryer to 200 C. Cook the sausage rolls for about 10 minutes or until they become golden and are puffed. Serve immediately with tomato relish.

19   GARLIC-ROSEMARY BRUSSELS SPROUTS

- This Brussels sprouts recipe will surely be your go-to side dish for lunch on busy days. It's healthy and easy to prepare, and it doesn't take much time or effort to make.
- Preparation Time: 10 minutes
- Cooking Time: 15 minutes

Servings: 4

Per serving:

Kcal: 180; Fat: 18g; Carbs: 15g; Protein: 12g; Sugars: 8g; Fibre: 6g

Ingredients:

- ½kg Brussels sprouts, trimmed and halved
- 3 tsp. olive oil
- 2 garlic cloves, minced
- 2 tsp. fresh rosemary
- ½ tsp. salt
- ¼ tsp. pepper
- 8 to 10 tsp. breadcrumbs

Instructions:

- Step 1: Preheat the air fryer to 176 C.
- Step 2: Toss the Brussels sprouts with garlic, salt, pepper, and 2 tablespoons of oil. Place the Brussels sprouts on a tray in the air-fryer basket and cook for 4 to 5 minutes. Stir the sprouts and cook again for 8 minutes until they are lightly browned, stirring halfway through the cooking time.
- Step 3: Toss the breadcrumbs with rosemary and sprinkle over the sprouts. Continue cooking for 3 more minutes until the crumbs are browned and the sprouts are tender. Serve immediately.

20 BREAD PUDDING

- This bread pudding is a fun dish, thanks to the chocolate that makes it different from the traditional pudding recipes. It is a rich and comforting dessert but low in calories.
- Preparation Time: 15 minutes
- Cooking Time: 15 minutes

Servings: 4

Per serving:

Kcal: 590; Fat: 38g; Carbs: 81g; Protein: 32g; Sugars: 28g; Fibre: 16g

Ingredients:

- 50g semisweet chocolate, chopped
- 25g half-and-half cream
- 25g sugar
- 50ml milk
- 1 large egg
- 1 tsp. vanilla extract
- ¼ tsp. salt
- 4 slices of bread, crusts removed, cut into cubes.

Instructions:

- Step 1: Melt chocolate in a small microwave-safe bowl and stir until smooth. Add cream and stir well.
- Step 2: In another bowl, whisk egg, sugar, milk, vanilla, and salt. Add the chocolate mixture and stir well. Add the bread cubes and toss gently to coat evenly. Let the mixture stand for 15 minutes.
- Step 3: Preheat the air fryer to 176 C. Spoon the bread mixture into a greased tray.
- Step 4: Place on the shelf in the air-fryer basket and cook for 12 to 15 minutes or until the knife inserted in the middle comes out clean.

21 SMOKED GOUDA CHEESE EGGS

- These air fryer-baked eggs are everything you need on those busy workdays or when you just want to keep it quick and simple in the kitchen. Perfectly cooked eggs, topped with your favourite seasonings, make this a gourmet-style lunch yet very easy to prepare.
- Preparation Time: 4 minutes
- Cooking Time: 16 minutes

Servings: 4

Per serving:

Kcal: 240; Fat: 26g; Carbs: 27g; Protein: 10g; Sugars: 16g; Fibre: 8g

Ingredients:

- 4 boiled eggs
- 6 to 8 tbsp. smoked gouda, chopped or grated cheese
- Seasoning of your choice
- Salt and pepper to taste
- 4 muffin cups.

Instructions:

- Step 1: Spray the inside of each muffin cup with oil. Add one boiled egg to each cup, and then, add 2 tbsp. of grated gouda cheese to each. Sprinkle salt and pepper to taste.
- Step 2: Sprinkle the seasonings of your choice on top of each cup.
- Step 3: Place the muffin cups into the air fryer basket and cook for 16 minutes at 176 C.

22 POPCORN SHRIMP TACOS

- This recipe combines classic flavours in new and healthy ways. The combination of crispy popcorn shrimp and tacos will surely turn out to be your family's favourite.
- Preparation Time: 10 minutes
- Cooking Time: 20 minuts

Servings: 4

Per serving:

Kcal: 450; Fat: 36g; Carbs: 27g; Protein: 10g; Sugars: 12g; Fibre: 8g

Ingredients:

- 200g coleslaw mix
- 1 bunch fresh cilantro
- 2 tsp. lime juice
- 2 tsp. honey
- ¼ tsp. salt
- 1 jalapeno pepper, seeded and minced, optional
- 2 large eggs
- 2 tsp. milk
- 100g all-purpose flour
- 50g breadcrumbs
- 1 tsp. ground cumin
- 1 tsp. garlic powder
- 1kg shrimp, peeled and deveined.

Instructions:

- Step 1: In a bowl, combine coleslaw mix, honey, cilantro, lime juice, salt, and if desired, jalapeno. Then toss to coat well. Set aside.
- Step 2: Preheat the air fryer to 176 C. In another bowl, whisk eggs, and add milk. Place the flour in a separate bowl. In another bowl, mix breadcrumbs, cumin powder, and garlic powder. Dip the shrimp in flour to coat both sides and shake off excess. Dip them in the egg mixture, and then in the breadcrumb mixture.
- Step 3: Arrange shrimp on a greased tray in a single layer and place it in the air-fryer basket. Spray with cooking oil. Cook for 10 minutes. Serve with coleslaw mix.

23 BACON-WRAPPED AVOCADO WEDGES

- Almost everything gets improved with this bacon and avocado dish. Since it's prepared in an air fryer, this appetizer is also healthier and tastes.
- Preparation Time: 10 minutes
- Cooking Time: 15 minuts

Servings: 4

Per serving:

Kcal: 140; Fat: 16g; Carbs: 12g; Protein: 6g; Sugars: 6g; Fibre: 4g

Ingredients:

- 2 avocados
- 12 bacon strips
- 8 tsp. mayonnaise
- 2 to 3 tsp. hot chilli sauce
- 1 to 2 tsp. lime juice.

Instructions:

- Step 1: Preheat the air fryer to 180 C. Cut each avocado in halves and remove the pit and peel. Then, cut each half into 3 parts. Gently wrap one bacon slice around one avocado wedge.
- Step 2: Place the wedges on the tray in an air-fryer basket in a single layer and cook for 10 to 15 minutes.
- Step 3: Meanwhile, in a bowl, stir mayonnaise, hot sauce, and lime juice. Serve wedges with sauce.

24 WHOLE CHICKEN

- This whole chicken recipe offers a wholesome meal. You can enjoy it for your lunch as well as dinner. It provides loads of protein and other nutrients making it a healthy option to include in your diet.
- Preparation Time: 10 minutes
- Cooking Time: 50 minut

Servings: 4

Per serving:

Kcal: 150; Fat: 26g; Carbs: 16g; Protein: 8g; Sugars: 10g; Fibre: 6g

Ingredients:

- 2kg pound whole chicken
- 1 tsp. olive oil
- 1 tsp. kosher salt or to taste
- ½ tsp. paprika
- ½ tsp. garlic powder
- ¼ tsp. black pepper
- ⅙ tsp. dried thyme leaves

Instructions:

- Step 1: First, dab the chicken dry and ensure the cavity is empty. Rub the skin with very little olive oil and sprinkle the seasoning.
- Step 2: Place the chicken into the air fryer basket breast-side down and cook for 30 minutes at 190 C.
- Step 3: Flip the chicken over and cook for another 20 minutes.
- Step 4: Remove from the air fryer and rest for 10 to 15 minutes before cutting. Serve immediately with spicy radishes.

25 PUMPKIN BISCUITS WITH SPICED APPLE BUTTER

- This one's a perfect recipe for your dinner when you want to keep it quick and simple. It tastes delicious and is easier to digest.
- Preparation Time: 10 minutes
- Cooking Time: 10 minutes

Servings: 4

Per serving:

Kcal: 180; Fat: 16g; Carbs: 18g; Protein: 8g; Sugars: 8g; Fibre: 6g

Ingredients:

- 100g all-purpose flour
- 25g packed brown sugar
- 1 tsp. cinnamon powder
- 2-½ tsp. baking powder
- 3/4 tsp. salt
- 2 tsp. unsalted butter
- 1 small pumpkin
- 1 tsp. Apple butter

Instructions:

- Step 1: Preheat the air fryer to 170 C. In a bowl, whisk the flour, brown sugar, cinnamon powder, baking powder, and salt.
- Step 2: Add in butter and mix well until the mixture resembles coarse crumbs. Then, add pumpkin and stir just until slightly moistened.
- Step 3: Turn the mixture onto a floured surface and knead gently 8 to 10 times. Roll the dough to 4-cm thickness. Then cut with a floured biscuit cutter.
- Step 4: Place the cut pieces of the dough in the greased air fryer in a single layer. Cook for 7 to 9 minutes or until golden brown. Serve with apple butter.

26 APPLE DANISH

- An air fryer makes this easy Apple Danish recipe healthier and yet just as delicious as your old-style fritter. It is a quick and easy dessert, which includes a yummy brown-butter glaze!
- Preparation Time: 10 minutes
- Cooking Time: 10 minute

Servings: 4

Per serving:

Kcal:190; Fat: 24g; Carbs: 27g; Protein: 16g; Sugars: 12g; Fibre: 6g

Ingredients:

- 100g all-purpose flour
- 25g sugar
- 2 tsp. baking powder
- 1½ tsp. ground cinnamon
- ½ tsp. salt
- 50ml milk
- 2 eggs
- 1 tsp. lemon juice
- 1½ tsp. vanilla extract
- 2 apples, peeled and chopped
- Cooking spray
- 4 tsp. butter
- 10 tsp. confectioners' sugar
- 1 tsp. milk

Instructions:

- Step 1: Preheat the air fryer to 250 C. In a bowl, combine flour, baking powder, cinnamon sugar, and salt. Add eggs, milk, lemon juice, and vanilla extract and stir until moistened. Fold in the apples.
- Step 2: Line the air-fryer basket with parchment and spritz with cooking spray. Drop the dough by 4 spoonsful onto the parchment and spritz with cooking spray. Cook for 5 to 6 minutes until golden brown. Turn the fritters and continue to air-fry for another 5 minutes.
- Step 3: Melt butter in a saucepan over medium heat. Cook carefully until the butter starts to brown. Remove from heat and allow to cool slightly. Add milk, confectioners' sugar, and browned butter in a bowl. Whisk until smooth. Drizzle over the fritters before serving.

27 CHICKEN TACO POCKETS

- Your family will love this delicious dish that's full of proteins. It tastes great and is a good stress reliever after a hectic day.
- Preparation Time: 10minutes
- Cooking Time: 20 minutes

Servings: 4

Per serving:

Kcal: 360; Fat: 18g; Carbs: 17g; Protein: 10g; Sugars: 6g; Fibre: 4g

Ingredients:

- 1kg ground beef
- 1 onion, chopped
- 4 tsp. shredded cheddar cheese
- 3 tsp. salsa
- 3 tsp. chopped green chillis
- ¼ tsp. garlic powder
- ¼ tsp. hot pepper sauce
- 1/8 tsp. salt
- 1/8 tsp. ground cumin
- 1 tube refrigerated crescent rolls

Instructions:

- Step 1: Preheat the air fryer to 176 C. In a skillet, cook onion and beef over medium heat until the meat is no longer pink. Crumble the meat and drain.
- Step 2: Stir in salsa, cheese, chillis, hot pepper sauce, garlic powder, salt, and cumin.
- Step 3: Unroll the crescent roll dough and separate it into 4 rectangles. Gently press perforations to seal. Place a small quantity of the meat mixture in the middle of each rectangle. Bring the corners to the centre and gently twist. Pinch to seal
- Step 4: Place the rolls on a greased tray in the air-fryer basket in a single layer and cook for 18 to 20 minutes. Serve with the toppings of your choice with a dessert of your choice. This dish goes well with apple Danish.

28 OREGANO POTATO CHIPS

- Oregano potato chips can be great to serve to your guests as a side dishzYou can also eat it for your mid-meal snacks.
- Preparation Time: 5 minutes
- Cooking Time: 10 minutes

Servings: 4

Per serving:

Kcal: 140; Fat: 8g; Carbs: 10g; Protein: 5g; Sugars: 6g; Fibre: 2g

Ingredients:

- 2 large potatoes
- Cooking spray
- ½ tsp. sea salt
- 5 tsp. oregano, optional

Instructions:

- Step 1: Preheat the air fryer to 180 C. Peel and cut potatoes into very thin slices. Transfer them to another bowl and add enough ice water to cover them. Soak for 15 minutes and drain.
- Step 2: Place the potato slices on a towel and gently pat dry. Spritz them with cooking spray and sprinkle salt and oregano.
- Step 3: Place the potato slices on a greased tray in an air-fryer basket in a single layer and cook for 8 to 10 minutes, stirring and turning midway through.

29 TAILGATE SAUSAGES

- Tailgate sausage is a filling recipe that will help you feel satisfied without experiencing any heaviness or bloating in the stomach. It is easy to digest and contains very less oil.
- Preparation Time: 10 minutes
- Cooking Time: 20 minute

Servings: 4

Per serving:

Kcal: 280; Fat: 16g; Carbs: 17g; Protein: 12g; Sugars: 10g; Fibre: 7g

Ingredients:

- 1kg beef flank steak
- 50g rice vinegar
- 10 tsp. soy sauce
- 20g brown sugar
- 2 tsp. ginger, grated
- 6 garlic cloves, minced
- 3 tsp. sesame oil
- 2 tsp. chili sauce
- ½ tsp. cornstarch

Instructions:

- Step 1: Cut beef into 2-cm thick strips. In a bowl, whisk the remaining ingredients until blended. Pour the marinade into a dish. Add beef and turn gently to coat. Cover and refrigerate for 2 to 8 hours.
- Step 2: Preheat the air fryer to 220 C. Drain the beef, discarding the marinade in a dish. Thread it onto 12 skewers that fit into your air fryer. Arrange the skewers in a single layer on a greased tray in the air-fryer basket and cook for 20 minutes or until the meat reaches the desired doneness.

30 SPICY RADISHES

- Radishes aren't only for salads anymore. These spicy radishes make colourful side dishes for any meal. Plus, they are quick to make in your air fryer.
- Preparation Time: 10 minutes
- Cooking Time: 15 minutes

Servings: 4
Per serving:

Kcal: 80; Fat: 5g; Carbs: 6g; Protein: 4g; Sugars: 2g; Fibre: 2g

Ingredients:

- 1kg radishes, trimmed and cut into thin slices
- 3 tsp. olive oil
- 1 tsp. dried oregano
- 1 tsp. Rosemary
- 1 tsp. ginger powder
- ¼ tsp. salt
- 1/8 tsp. pepper

Instructions:

- Step 1: Preheat the air fryer to 175 C. Toss the radishes with the remaining ingredients.
- Step 2: Place the radishes on a greased tray in the air-fryer basket and cook for 12 to 15 minutes or until crisp-tender, stirring occasionally.

Please scan the QR code below to access your bonus PDF with all 150 recipes with full coloured photos & beautiful designs alongside! This is the only way we can get the recipes with coloured photos to you & keep the book as reasonably priced as possible.

Also, once downloaded you can take the PDF with you digitally wherever you go- meaning you can cook these recipes wherever you may be! (As long as you have an air fryer!)

We hope you enjoy and do let us know your feedback!

STEP BY STEP Guide To Access-

1. Open Your Phones (Or Any Device You Want The Book On) Back Camera. The Back Camera Is The One You use as if you are taking a picture of someone.
2. Simply point your Camera at the QR code and 'tap' the QR code with your finger to focus the camera.
3. A link / pop up will appear. Simply tap that (and make sure you have internet connection) and the
4. FREE PDF containing all of the coloured images should appear.
5. Now you have access to these FOREVER. Simply 'Bookmark' The tab it opened on, or download the document and take wherever you want.
6. Repeat this on any device you want it on! (If you want it on a laptop, simply email the document to yourself!)
7. Any issues please email us at *vicandersonpublishing@gmail.com* and we will be happy to help!!

04

SECTION 4

DINNER RECIPES

01   STUFFED CHICKEN

- Stuffed chicken goes great as your main dish. It can be filling and is great to destress yourself after a long and stressful day.
- Preparation Time: 10 minutes
- Cooking Time: 15 minutes

Servings: 4

Per serving:

Kcal: 380; Fat: 25g; Carbs: 26g; Protein: 24g; Sugars: 12g; Fibre: 10g

Ingredients:

- 1kg boneless, skinless chicken breasts
- 4 tbsp. pesto
- 4 tbsp. goat cheese
- 1 tbsp. olive oil
- 1 tsp. salt
- 1 tsp. pepper
- 4 slices of prosciutto or any other meat of your choice
- 50g green beans, trimmed
- 2 cloves garlic, thinly sliced
- Tomato sauce for serving

Instructions:

- Step 1: Insert a thin knife into the middle part of the chicken breast and move gently back and forth to create 2-cm pockets.
- Step 2: Divide the pesto and goat cheese among the pockets using a spoon and rub with oil. Season with salt and pepper.
- Step 3: Lay prosciutto slices on a cutting board. Place chicken on the top and wrap the prosciutto around the chicken.
- Step 4: Place it in the air fryer basket seam-side down and air-fry at 176 C for 10 minutes.
- Step 5: Toss the green beans and garlic with salt and pepper. Move the chicken to one side of the fryer and place the green beans on the other side. Continue air-frying for 5 more minutes and serve together.

02 LEMON PEPPER CHICKEN THIGH

- Prepaing Lemon Pepper Chicken Thighs in your air fryer will soon become your easy dinner recipe. With very few ingredients, these chicken thighs are ready in just 20 minutes.
- Preparation Time: 10 minutes
- Cooking Time: 15 minutes

Servings: 4

Per serving:

Kcal: 290; Fat: 35g; Carbs: 26g; Protein: 24g; Sugars: 10g; Fibre: 7g

Ingredients:

- 1kg boneless skinless chicken thighs
- 1 tsp. olive oil
- 2½ tsp. lemon pepper butter sauce
- 1½ tsp. garlic powder
- Lemon pepper butter sauce
- 2 tsp. butter
- 1½ tsp. lemon juice and pepper mixture
- 4 tsp. dry lemon zest
- 2 tsp. salt
- 1½ tsp. black pepper
- 1½ tsp. garlic powder

Instructions:

- Step 1: Marinate the chicken. Mix all the ingredients for the seasoning in a bowl and set it aside.
- Step 2: Pat dry the chicken thighs with a paper towel and place them in another bowl. Add half of the lemon pepper seasoning blend, garlic powder, and oil.
- Step 3: Toss the chicken in the seasoning until well coated with the marinade. Allow to marinade for 30 minutes in the refrigerator.
- Step 4: Place the seasoned chicken thighs in the air fryer and cook at 200 C for 15 minutes, flipping halfway through.
- Step 5: Mix butter and the remaining lemon pepper seasoning. Brush lemon pepper mix and butter all over the chicken and serve.

03 AIR-FRIED VEGETABLES

- Air Fried Vegetables is an easy-to-prepare marinated and delicious vegetable recipe made just perfect in the air fryer. You will love how quick and tasty these roasted vegetables turn out.
- Preparation Time: 10 minutes
- Cooking Time: 15 minutes

Servings: 4

Per serving:

Kcal: 190; Fat: 15g; Carbs: 16g; Protein: 10g; Sugars: 8g; Fibre: 4g

Ingredients:

- 2 courgettes
- 1 red bell pepper
- 1 red onion
- 2 carrots
- 50g broccoli florets
- 1 tsp. oil
- 1 tsp. Italian seasoning
- 1 tsp. garlic powder
- ½ tsp. salt
- ¼ tsp. white pepper

Instructions:

- Step 1: Wash and cut the vegetables. Let the veggies sit in a colander to drain.
- Step 2: Add salt, oil, and seasoning and toss to coat the vegetables evenly.
- Step 3: Let the vegetables marinate for 15 minutes.
- Step 4: Place the marinated vegetables in the air fryer, and cook at 200 C for 15 minutes, tossing at 5 minutes intervals. Serve with stuffed chicken, cinnamon tortilla chips, or steak kabab.

04 BACON CHEESE SANDWICH

- Bacon sandwich is very easy to make and worth the calories when eaten taken in moderation.
- Preparation Time: 5 minutes
- Cooking Time: 7 minutes

Servings: 4

Per serving:

Kcal: 310; Fat: 15g; Carbs: 18g; Protein: 10g; Sugars: 6g; Fibre: 8g

Ingredients:

- 6 slices of bread
- 12 slices cheese
- 8 tsp. bacon crumbles
- 4 tsp. butter.

Instructions:

- Step 1: Place 2 slices of cheese next to the slice of bread. Cut one-third of the cheese slices into two equal parts and place each half near the outer edge of the bread slice.
- Step 2: Put 2 teaspoons of bacon crumbles in the middle. Cover with another slice of bread.
- Step 3: Spread butter on the top of the sandwich and place it in the air fryer basket with its side topped with butter facing down. Now, spread some more butter on the top side.
- Step 4: Repeat the process for the next set of bread slices.
- Step 5: Air fry for 4 minutes at 200 C and gently flip over. Toast for another 3 minutes and serve.

05 CRACKED GREEN BEANS

- this cracked green beans recipe makes up for a delicious side dish to your main course. It is tasty and tempting and can be prepared in just 15 minutes.
- Preparation Time: 5 minutes
- Cooking Time: 10 minute

Servings: 4

Per serving:

Kcal: 120; Fat: 10g; Carbs: 6g; Protein: 4g; Sugars: 4g; Fibre: 2g

Ingredients:

- ½kg green beans
- 6 strips of bacon
- 1 tsp. garlic powder
- ¼ tsp. black pepper
- 1 tsp. brown sugar
- 2-3 tsp. soy sauce

Instructions:

- Step 1: Place the green beans in a bowl and add soy sauce. Mix garlic and brown sugar and toss to coat well.
- Step 2: Add bacon to the seasoned green beans and mix to combine well. Transfer to the air fryer basket and cook for 10 minutes at 200 C.

06 CHEESEBURGER

- An air fryer cheeseburger is a perfect dinner menu for you when you want things done quickly without much mess. It's made with burger buns and hamburger patties and provides a good amount of protein.
- Preparation Time: 5 minutes
- Cooking Time: 15 minute

Servings: 4
Per serving:

Kcal: 450; Fat: 35g; Carbs: 26g; Protein: 24g; Sugars: 14g; Fibre: 12g

Ingredients:

- 4 hamburger patties
- ¼ tsp. salt
- ¼ tsp. black pepper
- ½ tsp. garlic powder
- 4 slices cheese
- 4 burger buns
- 4 rings from freshly cut onions
- 4 slices of tomatoes
- 2 leaves of lettuce

Instructions:

- Step 1: Mix salt, garlic powder, and black pepper. Sprinkle some mixture on one side of each burger patty.
- Step 2: Place the patties in the air fryer basket with its seasoned side down.
- Step 3: Sprinkle the remaining seasoning on the other side and allow to cook at 176 C for 12 to 15 minutes.
- Step 4: Once the burgers are well cooked, place the cheese slices on the top of each patty and slide the basket back into the fryer. Allow the residual heat in the fryer to melt the cheese.
- Step 5: Remove the patties from the air fryer. Spread some burger sauce on one side of the bun. Place lettuce, the cheeseburger, the tomato, and onion slices, then serve.

07 HERBED BRUSSELS SPROUTS

- It is a simple recipe that can be prepared with very little effort. Brussels sprouts will surely make up for the proteins that are often missing from your plant-based vegan dinner menu.It will take care of your body's needs for nutrients and help you stay fit and healthy while following a vegan lifestyle.
- Preparation Time: 10minutes
- Cooking Time: 8 minute

Servings: 4

Per serving:

Kcal: 100; Fat: 6g; Carbs: 15g; Protein: 10g; Sugars: 3g; Fibre: 4g

Ingredients:

- 100g Brussels sprouts, trimmed
- ½ tsp. dried thyme
- 1 tsp. garlic powder
- 1 tsp. dried parsley
- 2 tsp. oil
- ½ tsp. salt

Instructions:

- Step 1: Remove the outer leaves of the Brussels sprouts that do not appear fresh or healthy. Blanch the sprouts by boiling them for 10 to 15 minutes, Trim the sprouts and cut them into halves.
- Step 2: Place all ingredients in a mixing bowl and toss well to ensure the Brussels sprouts are coated evenly.
- Step 3: Pour them into the basket of the air fryer and cook for 8 to 10 minutes at 176 C.
- Step 4: Cool slightly and serve.

08 CINNAMON TORTILLA CHIPS

- Cinnamon Tortilla Chips are golden-brown and crispy with just the right amount of crunchiness and sweetness.
- Preparation Time: 5 minutes
- Cooking Time: 6 minutes

Servings: 4

Per serving:

Kcal: 240; Fat: 15g; Carbs: 15g; Protein: 10g; Sugars: 8g; Fibre: 7g

Ingredients:

- 2 tortilla wraps
- 25g granulated sugar
- 1 tsp. unsalted butter melted
- 1 tsp. ground cinnamon

Instructions:

- Step 1: Combine the sugar and cinnamon in a medium bowl, stirring together. Set the cinnamon sugar mixture aside.
- Step 2: Lay the tortilla wraps on a flat surface and brush the top of each with melted butter.
- Step 3: Sprinkle cinnamon sugar mixture over the tortilla wraps. Slice the tortilla wraps into triangles with a pizza cutter.
- Step 4: Place them into the air fryer basket lined with a sheet.
- Step 5: Air fry for 6 to 8 minutes at 176 C.

09 STEAK KABAB

- This is a quick and easy dish that can be used as a main dish or an appetizer. You can choose your favourite cut of steak, vegetables, red onion, and light seasonings to prepare this delicious recipe in just a few minutes.
- Preparation Time: 5 minutes
- Cooking Time: 6 minutes

Servings: 4

Per serving:

Kcal: 150; Fat: 10g; Carbs: 10g; Protein: 8g; Sugars: 4g; Fibre: 3g

Ingredients:

- 50g steak
- 1 green bell pepper
- 1 red bell pepper
- 1 red onion
- 1 tsp. olive oil
- 2 tsp. soy sauce

Instructions:

- Step 1: Preheat the air fryer to 180 C. Spray the air fryer basket with olive oil.
- Step 2: Cut the steak into bite-sized cubes and soak them in the soy sauce. Cut the vegetables into bite-sized pieces.
- Step 3: Add the steak, onion, and peppers to the skewer and repeat until you have reached its end.
- Step 4: Place the steak skewers in the prepared air fryer basket in a single layer. Cook for 10 minutes, flipping the skewers after about 5 minutes.

10 GRILLED PINEAPPLE

- Sweet and delicious, this juicy fruit can be used to prepare a refreshing dessert together with brown sugar, butter, vanilla, and cinnamon.
- Preparation Time: 5 minutes
- Cooking Time: 10 minutes

Servings: 4

Per serving:

Kcal: 320; Fat: 18g; Carbs: 26g; Protein: 10g; Sugars: 12g; Fibre: 7g

Ingredients:

- 1 pineapple, peeled and cut into thin slices
- 50g brown sugar
- 6 tbsp. unsalted butter
- 50g cup sugar
- 2 tsp. vanilla
- 1 tsp. cinnamon

Instructions:

- Step 1: Place the pineapple slices into a large bowl.
- Step 2: Pour the butter into the bowl. Toss the pineapple until all of the slices are well coated.
- Step 3: Add in the cinnamon, sugars, and vanilla. Toss the slices until they are evenly coated.
- Step 4: Place the pineapple slices into the air fryer basket and cook at 180 C for 10 minutes.

11   BAKED OATS

- Baked Oats is another fibre-rich recipe that is easy to digest and quick to prepare.
- Preparation Time: 20 minutes
- Cooking Time: 5 minutes

Servings: 4

Per serving:

Kcal: 315; Fat: 23g; Carbs: 18g; Protein: 16g; Sugars: 8g; Fibre: 7g

Ingredients:

- 1 banana
- 50g rolled oats
- 1 tsp. honey
- 1 tsp. vanilla extract
- ½ tsp. baking powder
- 1 egg
- 50ml cup milk
- ½ tsp. ground nutmeg

Instructions:

- Step 1: Grease the baking dish and keep it aside. Add all the ingredients into a blender and blend until smooth.
- Step 2: Pour the oats batter into the prepared baking dish.
- Step 3: Place it in the air fryer and bake at 165 C for 13 to 15 minutes.

12   LOADED BURRITO

- Loaded Burrito is a quick but delicious dinner recipe that comes out much better when made in the air fryer.
- Preparation Time: 20 minutes
- Cooking Time: 5 minutes

Servings: 4

Per serving:

Kcal: 315; Fat: 23g; Carbs: 18g; Protein: 16g; Sugars: 8g; Fibre: 7g

Ingredients:

- 4 tortilla wraps
- Second protein (ground chicken, ham, or bacon)
- 1 pack ground sausage
- 2 purple (or red) onions, diced
- 2 red potatoes, diced
- 2 green, red, and yellow bell peppers, diced
- 1 tsp. pepper
- 6 to 8 eggs
- ½ tsp. salt
- ½ tsp. garlic powder
- 8 to 10 tbsp. shredded cheese
- 1 tsp. Italian seasoning
- 2 tbsp. olive oil
- 2 tbsp. butter

Instructions:

- Step 1: Melt butter over medium heat and add olive oil. Add potatoes and toss for about 8 minutes before adding in bell peppers and onions. Sauté for 3 to 4 minutes. Remove from heat and set aside.
- Step 2: Cook proteins. Drain and set aside.
- Step: Scramble the eggs and season them with salt and pepper.
- Step 3: Now, start by placing the scrambled eggs in the centre of each tortilla wrap. Mash down lightly with the back of a spoon to hold the remaining ingredients. Add the proteins, veggies, and sautéed potatoes, and top with cheese.
- Step 4: Roll each burrito tightly and place into the basket of the air fryer. Spray with cooking spray.
- Step 5: Cook for 5 to 6 minutes at 176 C. Remove and serve.

13 AVOCADO DELIGHT

- Avocado Delight provides a good source of several vitamins and omega-3 fatty acids. Plus, it's also delicious and great to satisfy your craving for sugars.
- Preparation Time: 5 minutes
- Cooking Time: 20 minute

Servings: 4

Per serving:

Kcal: 240; Fat: 16; Carbs: 18g; Protein: 12g; Sugars: 6g; Fibre: 4g

Ingredients:

- 4 avocados, peeled and cut into strips or cubes
- 6 tbsp. unsalted butter
- 50g sugar
- 2 tsp. vanilla
- 1 tsp. cinnamon

Instructions:

- Step 1: Place the avocado cubes into a bowl. Pour the butter into the bowl. Toss the avocado until all of the cubes are well coated.
- Step 2: Add in the remaining ingredients. Toss the slices until they are evenly coated.
- Step 3: Place the avocado cubes into the air fryer basket and cook at 180 C for 10 minutes.

14 HOT DOGS

- These hot dogs will come out perfectly well when cooked in your air fryer. You will love the juicy flavours and surely devour them faster than ever.
- Preparation Time: 3 minutes
- Cooking Time: 5 minutes

Servings: 4

Per serving:

Kcal: 290; Fat: 12; Carbs: 28g; Protein: 10g; Sugars: 10g; Fibre: 6g

Ingredients:

- 4 hot dogs
- 4 tsp. mayonnaise
- 4 hot dog buns

Instructions:

- Step 1: Line the air fryer basket with parchment paper. Place 4 hot dogs on the air fryer basket in a single layer and cook for 4 to 5 minutes at 190 C. If you want the buns to be crispy, you can add the hot dog buns to the basket during the last minute of cooking time.
- Step 2: Remove the hotdogs from the fryer and place them in the hot dog buns.
- Step 3: Top with a tablespoon of mayonnaise and serve..

15 CORN DOGS

- Corn dogs can be a great side dish or an appetizer when you want to make an elaborate dinner. It's a quick and easy snack that is also easy to digest.
- Preparation Time: 4 minutes
- Cooking Time: 9 minutes

Servings: 4

Per serving:

Kcal: 230; Fat: 16; Carbs: 18g; Protein: 12g; Sugars: 6g; Fibre: 4g

Ingredients:

- 4 corn dogs
- 4 tsp. garlic mayonnaise

Instructions:

- Step 1: Preheat the air fryer to 180 C. Then line the basket with parchment paper.
- Step 2: Place the corn dogs in the preheated basket in a single layer and cook for 7 minutes. After 4 minutes, flip the corn dogs, and cook for 2 minutes.
- Step 3: Serve with garlic mayonnaise or any other dips and condiments of your choice.

16 GARLIC BUTTER SHRIMP

- This delicious garlic and butter shrimp can be cooked in your air fryer in less than 10 minutes! This dish tastes yummy and is sure to make you feel hungry just by looking at it.
- Preparation Time: 5 minutes
- Cooking Time: 8 minutes

Servings: 4

Per serving:

Kcal: 210; Fat: 15; Carbs: 16g; Protein: 10g; Sugars: 6g; Fibre: 3g

Ingredients:

- 1kg shrimp, peeled and deveined
- 4 tbsp. butter
- 2 cloves garlic, minced

Instructions:

- Step 1: Remove the shells of the shrimps and rinse well. Pat them dry and place them in a large bowl. Set aside.
- Step 2: Pour the melted butter and minced garlic over the shrimp, and toss well, coating the shrimp with the mixture.
- Step 3: Add the shrimp to the air fryer basket and cook at 180 C for 6 to 8 minutes, tossing halfway through.

17   SPICY MUSK MELONS

- This fibre-rich fruit can be used as a yummy side dish that can also be great for those trying to lose weight.
- Preparation Time: 5 minutes
- Cooking Time: 10 minute

Servings: 4

Per serving:

Kcal: 290; Fat: 18; Carbs: 30g; Protein: 14g; Sugars: 10g; Fibre: 9g

Ingredients:

- 1 musk melon, peeled and cut into cubes
- 6 tbsp. unsalted butter
- 1 tsp. oregano
- 1 tsp. Rosemary
- 1 tsp. salt
- 1 tsp. pepper
- 2 tsp. vanilla
- 1 tsp. cinnamon

Instructions:

- Step 1: Place the musk melon cubes into a bowl.
- Step 2: Pour the butter into the bowl. Toss the musk melon until all the cubes are well coated.
- Step 3: Add in the remaining ingredients. Toss the cubes until they are evenly coated.
- Step 4: Place the musk melon into the air fryer basket and cook at 180 C for 10 minutes.

18 PIGS IN A BLANKET

- Pigs in a blanket are easy to prepare in your air fryer. They taste great and offer a good amount of proteins and other nutrients.
- Preparation Time: 5 minutes
- Cooking Time: 8 minutes

Servings: 4

Per serving:

Kcal: 190; Fat: 17; Carbs: 18g; Protein: 12g; Sugars: 4g; Fibre: 3g

Ingredients:

- 12 cocktail sausages
- 1 can of crescent rolls

Instructions:

- Step 1: Preheat the air fryer to 180 C. Open the crescent rolls and cut each sheet into three equal pieces.
- Step 2: Take one cocktail frank and wrap it with a piece of the crescent dough. Repeat the same for all cocktail franks.
- Step 3: Add the parchment paper to the basket of the air fryer and place the crescent dogs in it. Air fry for 3 to 4 minutes. Turn them and cook for an additional 3 to 4 minutes.

19 TEMPTING OREOS

- This air-fried Oreos dish is a delicious and easy treat that can be made in just a few minutes! It's a perfect dessert to prepare when you are short on time or are craving something sweet.
- Preparation Time: 5 minutes
- Cooking Time: 5 minutes

Servings: 4

Per serving:

Kcal: 90; Fat: 13; Carbs: 18g; Protein: 10g; Sugars: 8g; Fibre: 4g

Ingredients:

- 8 Oreos
- 8 crescents
- 4 tbsp. powdered sugar

Instructions:

- Step 1: Preheat the air fryer to 18 crescent rolls.
- Step 2: Line the air fryer basket with parchment paper.
- Step 3: Add the Oreos onto the air fryer basket forming a single layer and cook for 5 to 6 minutes.
- Step 4: Remove them from the air fryer and sprinkle the fried Oreos with powdered sugar. Serve immediately.

20 HONEY GLAZED CARROTS

- These tasty and delicious honey-glazed carrots can be cooked to perfection in your air fryer. This recipe provides a good source of vitamin A and vitamin E, while being very low in calories. This is what makes it so good for those trying to lose weight.
- Preparation Time: 5 minutes
- Cooking Time: 10 minutes

Servings: 4

Per serving:

Kcal: 70; Fat: 6; Carbs: 10g; Protein: 5g;
Sugars: 3g; Fibre: 2g

Ingredients:

- 10 large carrots
- 1 tsp. olive oil
- 1 tsp. honey
- 1 tsp. brown sugar
- ¼ tsp. salt
- ¼ tsp. pepper

Instructions:

- Step 1: Brush oil on the air fryer basket. Stir together the brown sugar, honey, salt, and pepper in a bowl.
- Step 2: Add the carrots, and coat them with the sugar and honey mixture.
- Step 3: Place the coated carrots in the air fryer basket and cook for 8 to 10 minutes.

21 SPICY CASHEWS

- This spicy and salty snack is too tasty to resist. If you are looking to prepare a quick side dish to go with your main dish for dinner, this one's just perfect. It tastes delicious and takes just 15 minutes to get ready.
- Preparation Time: 5 minutes
- Cooking Time: 10 minutes

Servings: 4

Per serving:

Kcal: 217; Fat: 17; Carbs: 20g; Protein: 16g; Sugars: 10g; Fibre: 8g

Ingredients:

- 4 tbsp. unsalted butter melted
- 100g cashew nuts, halved
- 1 tsp. garlic powder
- 1 tsp. onion powder
- 1 tsp. salt
- 1 tsp. black pepper

Instructions:

- Step 1: Preheat the air fryer to 176 C. Place the cashew nuts in a bowl and add melted butter.
- Step 2: Stir the cashew nuts to ensure they are well coated with butter so that the other ingredients can stick to them.
- Step 3: Stir in the remaining ingredients and toss the cashew nuts so that they are evenly covered.
- Step 4: Transfer them to the air fryer basket, and cook for 10 minutes, shaking the basket halfway through.

22 CHICKEN WINGS

- These chicken wings are too tempting and delicious to resist. Cooking them in your air fryer will give them an extra crispiness.
- Preparation Time: 5 minutes
- Cooking Time: 20 minutes

Servings: 4

Per serving:

Kcal: 490; Fat: 48; Carbs: 50g; Protein: 24g; Sugars: 18g; Fibre: 15g

Ingredients:

- 24 chicken wings
- 10ml olive oil
- 1 tbsp. black pepper
- 2 tsp. onion powder
- 2 tsp. garlic powder
- 8 to 10 tbsp. hot sauce

Instructions:

- Step 1: Preheat the air fryer to 180 C. Line the air fryer basket with parchment paper.
- Step 2: Add the chicken wings, seasonings, and olive oil in a sealable plastic bag. Then, seal the bag and gently toss the wings to coat them well with oil and seasonings.
- Step 3: Remove the wings from the bag and place them into the air fryer basket in a single layer. Cook for 18 minutes, flipping once every 5 to 6 minutes.
- Step 4: Add the cooked wings to a bowl and cover with the hot sauce. Toss the chicken wings to cover them completely and place them on a serving dish. Serve with fried yam or spicy capsicum fries.

23 GREMOLATA-TOPPED FISH FILLETS

- This delicious dish will surely pep up your mood and help you feel better by adding great taste and nutrients to your platter. With loads of healthy omega 3 fats, this recipe will help you keep your cholesterol levels in check.
- Preparation Time: 15 minutes
- Cooking Time: 20 minutes

Servings: 4

Per serving:

Kcal: 365; Fat: 26g; Carbs: 6g; Protein: 35g; Sugars:7g; Fibre: 3g

Ingredients:

- 2 tsp. olive oil, divided
- 1 clove garlic, crushed to a coarse paste
- 1kg medium-firm fish fillets (seabass, halibut, mahi-mahi, or swordfish), cut into 4 pieces
- 1 bunch of fresh parsley, chopped
- Finely grated zest
- Juice of 1 lemon
- 5 tbsp. crumbled plantain chips
- 1/4 tsp. sea salt

Instructions:

- Step 1: Preheat the air fryer to 176 C. Line a baking sheet with aluminium foil. Spread the 2 tablespoons of olive oil on top.
- Step 2: Mix plantain chip crumbs, lemon zest, garlic, parsley, and the remaining 1 tablespoon of olive oil.
- Step 3: Place the fish fillets on the shelf of your air fryer. Sprinkle lemon juice and salt.
- Step 4: Coat the top of the fish fillet with the crumb mixture evenly.
- Step 5: Bake for about 15 to 20 minutes, or until fish is well cooked.

24 HONEY AND PEPPER GLAZED PUMPKIN

- Honey and pepper glazed pumpkin will provide a rich fibre content to your meals and help ease your digestion while making your taste buds happier.
- Preparation Time: 5 minutes
- Cooking Time: 10 minutes

Servings: 4

Per serving:

Kcal: 88; Fat: 9; Carbs: 10g; Protein: 5g;
Sugars: 4g; Fibre: 3g

Ingredients:

- 1 tsp. olive oil
- 1 large pumpkin, cut into cubes
- 1 tsp. honey
- 1 tsp. brown sugar
- ¼ tsp. salt
- 1 tsp. pepper

Instructions:

- Step 1: Brush oil on the air fryer basket. Stir together the brown sugar, honey, salt, and pepper in a bowl.
- Step 2: Add the cubes of pumpkin, and coat them with the sugar and honey mixture.
- Step 3: Place the coated pumpkins in the air fryer basket and cook for 8 to 10 minutes.

25 BUFFALO ROASTED CAULIFLOWER

- This low-carb Buffalo Roasted Cauliflower recipe turns out perfectly crispy when prepared in the air fryer. This healthy version of fried cauliflower is full of flavours. You will surely love to prepare it for your lunch and dinner over and over again
- Preparation Time: 5 minutes
- Cooking Time: 15 minute

Servings: 4

Per serving:

270; Fat: 21g; Carbs: 24g; Protein: 13g;
Sugars: 10g; Fibre: 6g

Ingredients:

- 2 large cauliflowers, chopped
- 20ml Buffalo wing sauce
- 1 tsp. olive oil
- 1 tsp. garlic powder
- ½ tsp. salt
- 1 tsp. whole wheat flour
- 1 tsp. Buffalo wing sauce for serving.

Instructions:

- Step 1: In a bowl, add the cauliflower, olive oil, sauce, garlic powder, flour, and salt. Toss until the sauce coats the cauliflower evenly.
- Step 2: Spray the air fryer shelf with cooking spray and place the cauliflower mixture on it.
- Step 3: Set the air fryer to 200 C and cook for 15 minutes.

26 FRIED YAM

- Yam gets a makeover with this healthy but tasty recipe. Spicy fried yam is a great side dish for your lunch and dinner. Plus, it is quick to make in your air fryer.
- Preparation Time: 10 minutes
- Cooking Time: 15 minutes

Servings: 4

Per serving:

Kcal: 70; Fat: 8g; Carbs: 12g; Protein: 5g; Sugars: 6g; Fibre: 4g

Ingredients:

- 1kg yam, peeled and cut into thin slices
- 3 tsp. olive oil
- 1 tsp. dried oregano
- 1 tsp. Rosemary
- 1 tsp. onion powder
- 1 tsp. garlic powder
- ¼ tsp. salt
- 1/8 tsp. pepper

Instructions:

- Step 1: Preheat the air fryer to 175 C. Toss the yam with the remaining ingredients.
- Step 2: Place the yam on a greased tray in the air-fryer basket and cook for 12 to 15 minutes or until crisp-tender, stirring occasionally.

27 STEAK FAJITAS

- It's easy to make steak fajitas in the air fryer. You can season it with vegetables and air-fry it. It's a simple but restaurant-quality cooking at home!
- Preparation Time: 10 minutes
- Cooking Time: 20 minutes

Servings: 4

Per serving:

Kcal: 498; Fat: 38; Carbs: 50g; Protein: 25g; Sugars: 14g; Fibre: 13g

Ingredients:

- 1 red pepper, sliced crosswise
- 1 yellow pepper, sliced crosswise
- 1 red onion, sliced ½-cm thick
- 2 tsp. grated lime zest
- 2 tbsp. lime juice
- ¼ tsp. ground cumin
- 1 tbsp. canola oil
- ½ tsp. granulated garlic
- 1 tsp. salt
- 1 tsp. pepper
- ½kg skirt steak, crosswise cut into 10-cm pieces
- 1 tsp. chilli powder
- 1 bunch cilantro, chopped
- 4 tortilla wraps, warmed

Instructions:

- Step 1: In a bowl, toss the onion, peppers, lime zest and juice, garlic, cumin, salt, and pepper. Air-fry at 176 C for 10 minutes.
- Step 2: Meanwhile, rub the steak with some oil, add seasoning with chilli powder. Push the vegetables to one side of the air fryer and place the steak on the other side. Air fry for 10 minutes.
- Step 3: Transfer the steak to a cutting board and let it rest for 5 minutes before slicing. Toss the vegetables with cilantro. Fill the tortilla wraps with peppers and steak. Top with sour cream, sprinkle cilantro, and serve.

28 APPLE PIE TORTILLA WRAPS

- These delicious apple pie tortilla wraps are easy and quick to prepare. Plus, preparing them in your air fryer will also keep down the calories, making it a great option if you are looking to lose weight or keep your blood sugar levels in control.
- Preparation Time: 12 minutes
- Cooking Time: 8 minutes

Servings: 4

Per serving:

Kcal: 190; Fat: 35g; Carbs: 43g; Protein: 10g; Sugars: 12g; Fibre: 10g

Ingredients:

- 4 tortilla wraps
- 1 can apple pie filling of your choice
- 1/8 tsp. ground cinnamon
- ½ tsp. lemon juice
- 1 tbsp. all-purpose flour

Instructions:

- Step 1: Mix together the apple pie filling, lemon juice, cinnamon, and flour in a bowl. You can also create your own apple pie filling by steaming the apples in your air fryer for 5 minutes. Mash the apple and add 2 teaspoons sugar and cinnamon powder or any other flavourings of your choice to prepare your own apple pie filling.
- Step 2: Divide the mixture into sections. Add one scoop of the apple pie mixture into the middle of the tortilla wraps.
- Step 3: Using a very small amount of water, moisten the outer edges of the tortilla wraps with water. Fold each tortilla wrap carefully by rolling it over the filling. Moisten each edge with very little water to seal.
- Step 4: Preheat the air fryer to 476 C for 10 minutes. Place the tortilla wraps carefully into the shelf of the air fryer and cook for 8 to 10 minutes, flipping halfway through.
- Step 5: Remove from the air fryer and top with 1 teaspoon powdered sugar.

29 SPICY CAPSICUM FRIES

- These spicy capsicum fries are soft yet crunchy. They taste great and can be prepared quickly any time you are looking for a quick snack.
- Preparation Time: 10 minutes
- Cooking Time: 5 minutes

Servings: 4

Per serving:

Kcal: 120; Fat: 6; Carbs: 8g; Protein: 6g; Sugars: 3g; Fibre: 3g

Ingredients:

- 250g capsicum
- 50g flour
- ¼ tsp. salt
- 1 tsp. asafoetida
- 1 tsp. turmeric

Instructions:

- Step 1: Preheat the air fryer to 200 C.
- Step 2: Wash the capsicum and cut them into 2 halves. Remove the seeds. Cut each half into 3 to 4 vertical pieces.
- Step 3: In a bowl, add flour, salt, turmeric, and asafoetida. Place the capsicum pieces in the gram flour mixture and toss to cover them well.
- Step 4: Lay the capsicums in the air fryer basket and cook for 4 to 5 minutes.

30 CRAB CAKES

- Crab cakes made in the air fryer with crab meat and a variety of seasonings can be a flavourful appetizer. You can serve this dish to your family and guest to impress them with your cooking skills.
- Preparation Time: 5 minutes
- Cooking Time: 10 minutes

Servings: 4

Per serving:

Kcal: 180; Fat: 10; Carbs: 12g; Protein: 8g; Sugars: 5g; Fibre: 3g

Ingredients:

- 1kg lump crab meat
- 1 red bell pepper, chopped
- 3 onions, chopped
- 3 tsp. mayonnaise
- 3 tsp. breadcrumbs
- 2 tsp. black pepper
- 1 tsp. white pepper
- 1 tsp. ginger powder
- 1 tsp. garlic powder
- 1 tsp. lemon juice.

Instructions:

- Step 1: Preheat the air fryer to 176 C.
- Step 2: In a bowl, add the lump crab meat, bell pepper, onions, mayonnaise, breadcrumbs, seasoning, and lemon juice. Mix well until combined. Form 4 evenly-sized crab patties.
- Step 3: Place a piece of parchment paper inside the air fryer and then place each crab cake onto the paper. Cook the crab cakes in the fryer for 8 to 10 minutes or until the crust turns golden brown.
- Step 4: Remove the crab cakes carefully from your air fryer and serve with your favourite sauce!

31 SEASONED SPATCHCOCK CHICKEN

- If you love chicken, this recipe is perfect for you. It will satisfy your cravings and provide natural antioxidants and anti-inflammatory agents in the form of a rich blend of seasonings.
- Preparation Time: 10 minutes
- Cooking Time: 45 minutes

Servings: 4

Per serving:

Kcal: 198; Fat: 26g; Carbs: 10g; Protein: 16g; Sugars: 3g; Fibre: 4g

Ingredients:

- 1kg whole chicken
- 4 cloves garlic, crushed
- ½ tsp. chopped fresh rosemary
- 1 lemon, zested and juiced
- 2 tsp. chopped fresh oregano
- ½ tsp. chopped fresh thyme
- 2 tsp. avocado oil, divided
- 1 tsp. salt

Instructions:

- Step 1: Prepare the slurry for seasoning. Mix crushed garlic, lemon juice, chopped rosemary, lemon zest, chopped oregano, chopped thyme, salt, and 1 tablespoon of avocado oil.
- Step 2: Preheat the air fryer to 176 C.
- Step 3: Cut along the right side of the chicken's backbone using poultry all the way down the spine. Repeat the same on the left side to remove the backbone entirely.
- Step 4: Turn the chicken over and open it up to lie flat. You can flatten the chicken more thoroughly by pulling on one side and pushing it down on the other.
- Step 5: Place the chicken with its skin-side-up inside the prepared skillet.
- Step 6: Pat dry using a paper towel. Rub seasoning slurry over the skin side of the chicken.
- Step 7: Roast for about 45 minutes and allow to rest for 5 minutes in a pan before serving. This dish goes well with broiled asparagus.

32 SALT AND PEPPER BANANA CHIPS

- These salt and pepper banana chips can satisfy your craving for something tasty and crunchy. Prepared in the air fryer, these delicious snacks offer a healthier option to your deep-fried snacks.
- Preparation Time: 5 minutes
- Cooking Time: 10 minutes

Servings: 4

Per serving:

Kcal: 170; Fat: 14g; Carbs: 12g; Protein: 6g; Sugars: 6g; Fibre: 4g

Ingredients:

- 4 large raw bananas
- ½ tsp. salt
- 1 tsp. pepper

Instructions:

- Step 1: Preheat the air fryer to 180 C. Peel and cut bananas into very thin slices. Transfer them to another bowl and add enough ice water to cover them. Soak for 15 minutes and drain.
- Step 2: Place the banana slices on a towel and gently pat dry. Spritz them with cooking spray and sprinkle salt and pepper. Toss well to combine.
- Step 3: Place the banana slices on a greased tray in an air-fryer basket in a single layer and cook for 8 to 10 minutes, stirring and turning midway through.
- Step 4: Store in an air-tight container and eat a bowlful as and when you crave a healthy and tasty snack..

33 PICKLES

- This one's a great recipe that goes well as your side dish with rice, meat, vegetables, or any other dish on your dinner menu. It tastes great, does not need much preparation, and requires very less time.
- Preparation Time: 10 minutes
- Cooking Time: 6 minutes

Servings: 4

Per serving:

Kcal: 320; Fat: 27; Carbs: 30g; Protein: 12g; Sugars: 10g; Fibre: 6g

Ingredients:

- 36 pickle slices
- 1 cup breadcrumbs
- 1 egg
- ½ tsp. water
- 50g all-purpose flour
- ½ tsp. garlic powder
- ½ tsp. paprika
- ½ tsp. dried dill

Instructions:

- Step 1: Preheat the air fryer to 190 C.
- Step 2: Drain the pickles and lay them on a paper towel to dry them thoroughly.
- Step 3: In a shallow wide bowl, place breadcrumbs. In another bowl, whisk the egg and add water. In another bowl, whisk the flour, paprika, garlic powder, and dill.
- Step 4: Dredge the pickles through the flour mixture one by one and dip them in the egg mixture. Then, press them into the breadcrumb mixture to coat well.
- Step 5: Spray the air fryer basket with cooking oil and carefully place the coated pickles in a single layer. Lightly spray the top of the pickles and cook for 4 minutes. Flip them and cook them for an additional 2 to 4 minutes, until they are crispy and perfectly browned.

34 CHEESE CURDS

- Cheese curds will be your ultimate appetizer and a go-to dish when you want to prepare something tasty but healthy! It's also a delicious starter when served piping hot with your favourite dipping sauce.
- Preparation Time: 15 minutes
- Cooking Time: 30 minutes

Servings: 4

Per serving:

Kcal: 490; Fat: 37; Carbs: 34g; Protein: 20g; Sugars: 12g; Fibre: 10g

Ingredients:

- 90ml cheese curds
- 50g breadcrumbs
- 2 tsp. Italian seasoning
- ½ tsp. salt
- ¼ tsp. pepper
- 3 eggs
- 1 tsp. water
- 50g all-purpose flour

Instructions:

- Step 1: In a bowl, whisk the Italian seasoning, breadcrumbs, salt, and pepper. In another bowl, combine the water and eggs, whisking to combine well.
- Step 2: Place the cheese curds in the bowl and add flour. Toss gently to coat.
- Step 3: Dredge the curds through the eggs one by one and roll them in the breadcrumb mixture. Place the coated eggs on a plate.
- Step 4: Preheat the air fryer to 190 C. Place the breaded cheese curds in the air fryer basket. Spray the top with cooking oil and cook for 5 to 6 minutes.

35 CRUNCHY OKRA CHIPS

- These crunchy and spicy okra chips dipped in breadcrumbs can be too tempting to resist. You will relish the texture of crunchy okra bites every time you eat this snack.
- Preparation Time: 10 minutes
- Cooking Time: 8 minute

Servings: 4

Per serving:

Kcal: 108; Fat: 19; Carbs: 14g; Protein: 7g; Sugars: 5g; Fibre: 3g

Ingredients:

- 250g okra
- 50g breadcrumbs
- 1 tsp. salt
- ½ tsp. coriander powder
- ¼ tsp. cumin powder
- 1 egg
- 3 tsp. flour

Instructions:

- Step 1: Wash and pat dry okra on a paper towel. Cut the edges and discard. Make 2 pieces of each okra by cutting through vertically from top to bottom.
- Step 2: Mix breadcrumbs, cumin powder, and coriander powder in a bowl.
- Step 3: Put the flour in another bowl. Whisk one egg in the third bowl. Dip the okra pieces into the flour, then into the egg, and lastly, into the breadcrumbs.
- Step 4: Place the coated okra pieces in a single layer in your air fryer and cook for 7 to 9 minutes at 180 C, flipping halfway.

36 SPICY AUBERGINE

- This spicy aubergine recipe is so mouth-watering that you will have your family asking you for more. It's also a healthy dish as it requires very less oil when prepared in your air fryer.
- Preparation Time: 10 minutes
- Cooking Time: 8 minut

Servings: 4

Per serving:

Kcal: 120; Fat: 14; Carbs: 12g; Protein: 10g; Sugars: 6g; Fibre: 5g

Ingredients:

- 2 large aubergine
- ½ tsp. garlic powder
- 1 tsp. salt
- ¼ tsp. onion powder
- 50g flour
- 3 tsp. flour

Instructions:

- Step 1: Cut the aubergine to make thin slices, about ½ cm in thickness.
- Step 2: Mix flour, onion powder, and garlic powder in a bowl. Add water to make a thick paste.
- Step 3: Dip the aubergine slices into the paste. Place the coated aubergine in a single layer in your air fryer and cook for 7 to 9 minutes at 180 C, flipping halfway.

37 BACON-WRAPPED STUFFED JALAPENOS

- Roasted jalapeno is a fun-filled dish, thanks to its juice and creamy texture. Wrapped in thinly-sliced bacon, this one's the perfect party food for all occasions!
- Preparation Time: 10 minutes
- Cooking Time: 14 minutes

Servings: 4

Per serving:

Kcal: 199; Fat: 19; Carbs: 20g; Protein: 14g; Sugars: 11g; Fibre: 9g

Ingredients:

- 12 Jalapenos
- 12 slices of thinly cut bacon
- 25g cream cheese
- 25g shredded cheddar cheese
- ¼ tsp. garlic powder
- 1/8 tsp. onion powder
- Salt and pepper to taste

Instructions:

- Step 1: Cut the jalapenos into halves. Remove the stems, seeds, and membranes.
- Step 2: Add shredded cheddar cheese, cream cheese, onion powder, garlic powder, salt, and pepper in a bowl and mix.
- Step 3: Scoop the cream mixture into each jalapeno using a spoon, filling it until just below the top.
- Step 4: Preheat the air fryer to 176 C for 3 minutes.
- Step 5: Cut the bacon slices in halves. Wrap each half of the jalapeno in one piece of bacon.
- Step 6: Place these bacon-wrapped jalapenos in the air fryer in a single layer without overlapping. Air fry for 14 to 16 minutes or until the bacon is thoroughly cooked.

38 RAVIOLI

- This one's a delicious and healthier version of deep-fried snacks. It can be prepared with just 3 ingredients and can be stored in the freezer for up to 3 months!
- Preparation Time: 5 minutes
- Cooking Time: 6 minutes

Servings: 4

Per serving:

Kcal: 418; Fat: 29; Carbs: 30g; Protein: 16g; Sugars: 14g; Fibre: 10g

Ingredients:

- 12 raviolis, frozen
- 50ml buttermilk
- 50g breadcrumbs
- Hot sauce for dipping

Instructions:

- Step 1: Preheat the air fryer to 190 C.
- Step 2: Place 2 bowls side by side. Put the breadcrumbs in one and buttermilk in the other.
- Step 3: Then, dip the pieces of ravioli into the buttermilk. Remove from the buttermilk, and then dip the pieces in the breadcrumbs one by one, making sure they are well coated.
- Step 4: Place the breaded ravioli into the air fryer in a single layer and cook for 6 to 7 minutes.
- Step 5: Remove from the air fryer and serve immediately with hot sauce or store in the freezer for up to 3 months.

39 FRIED ELEPHANT YAM

- Fried elephant yam can be your answer to those who believe that nothing can taste better than potato chips and fries. It is tasty and tempting and can be made in just a few minutes.
- Preparation Time: 10 minutes
- Cooking Time: 8 minutes

Servings: 4

Per serving:

Kcal: 122; Fat: 19; Carbs: 10g; Protein: 9g; Sugars: 4g; Fibre: 3g

Ingredients:

- 1 large elephant yam
- ½ tsp. garlic powder
- ¼ tsp. onion powder
- 1 tsp. Salt
- 1 tsp. turmeric powder
- 50g flour
- 1 tsp. asafoetida
- 3 tsp. flour

Instructions:

- Step 1: Clean elephant yam well and cut it to make thin slices, about ½ cm in thickness.
- Step 2: Mix gram flour, onion powder, asafoetida, garlic powder, turmeric powder, and salt in a bowl. Add water to make a thick paste.
- Step 3: Dip elephant yam into the paste. Place the coated elephant yam in a single layer in your air fryer and cook for 7 to 9 minutes at 180 C, flipping halfway.

40 GARLIC PARMESAN WINGS

- This dish brings with itself the goodness of garlic, which is loaded with strong medicinal properties, thanks to its antioxidant, anti-inflammatory, and cholesterol-lowering effects.
- Preparation Time: 10 minutes
- Cooking Time: 30 minute

Servings: 4

Per serving:

Kcal: 560; Fat: 47; Carbs: 56g; Protein: 38g; Sugars: 20g; Fibre: 16g

Ingredients:

- 1kg chicken wings (flats and drums)
- 1 tsp. olive oil
- 1 1 tsp. baking powder
- 1 tsp. kosher salt
- 1 tsp. garlic powder
- 1 tsp. onion powder
- 1 tsp. paprika
- 1 tsp. black pepper
- 1 tsp. unsalted butter, melted
- 4 cloves garlic, minced
- 50g grated parmesan cheese

Instructions:

- Step 1: Pat the chicken wings dry with a paper towel and place them in a bowl. Drizzle olive oil, tossing gently to coat well.
- Step 2: In another bowl, combine the salt, baking powder, garlic powder, onion powder, pepper, and paprika. Sprinkle the mixture over the wings and toss gently to coat.
- Step 3: Preheat the air fryer to 190 C. Place the wings on the shelf of the air fryer a single layer with its skin side up and cook for 15 minutes. Flip the wings carefully and cook for another 5 to 8 minutes.
- Step 4: Meanwhile, add the butter in a microwave-safe bowl and melt it in a microwave. Stir in the parmesan and minced garlic. Remove the cooked chicken wings from the fryer and transfer to a bowl. Then, toss them with the garlic butter.

Please scan the QR code below to access your bonus PDF with all 150 recipes with full coloured photos & beautiful designs alongside! This is the only way we can get the recipes with coloured photos to you & keep the book as reasonably priced as possible.

Also, once downloaded you can take the PDF with you digitally wherever you go- meaning you can cook these recipes wherever you may be! (As long as you have an air fryer!)

We hope you enjoy and do let us know your feedback!

STEP BY STEP Guide To Access-

1. Open Your Phones (Or Any Device You Want The Book On) Back Camera. The Back Camera Is The One You use as if you are taking a picture of someone.
2. Simply point your Camera at the QR code and 'tap' the QR code with your finger to focus the camera.
3. A link / pop up will appear. Simply tap that (and make sure you have internet connection) and the
4. FREE PDF containing all of the coloured images should appear.
5. Now you have access to these FOREVER. Simply 'Bookmark' The tab it opened on, or download the document and take wherever you want.
6. Repeat this on any device you want it on! (If you want it on a laptop, simply email the document to yourself!)
7. Any issues please email us at *vicandersonpublishing@gmail.com* and we will be happy to help!!

05

SECTION 5

SNACKS

01   TORTILLA CHIPS

- Crispy and crunchy, these tortilla chips are sure to take your Mexican-inspired snacking menu to the next level.
- Preparation Time: 5 minutes
- Cooking Time: 5 minutes

Servings: 4

Per serving:

Kcal: 320; Fat: 23; Carbs: 28g; Protein: 13g; Sugars: 8g; Fibre: 5g

Ingredients:

- 4 10-cm long corn tortilla wraps
- Avocado oil for spray
- ½ tsp. salt

Instructions:

- Step 1: Preheat the air fryer to 180 C for 5 minutes.
- Step 2: Spray both sides of the tortilla wrap with oil. Sprinkle a little salt. Cut the tortilla wraps into triangles using a pizza cutter or a sharp knife.
- Step 3: Place these triangles in the air fryer basket in a single layer and air fry for 3 to 4 minutes. Then open the basket and flip the chips. Cook for another 1 or 2 minutes until they are golden brown and crispy.

02 LOADED TATER TOTS

- This one's a delicious appetizer that will boost your air fryer skills. This dish can be a great snack to satisfy your mid-meal hunger pangs.
- Preparation Time: 8 minutes
- Cooking Time: 8 minutes

Servings: 4

Per serving:

Kcal: 388; Fat: 37; Carbs: 40g; Protein: 29g; Sugars: 14g; Fibre: 10g

Ingredients:

- 100g tater tots
- 25g shredded cheddar cheese
- 1 to 1½ tsp. bacon bits
- 2 onions, chopped
- 2 tsp. sour cream

Instructions:

- Step 1: Preheat the air fryer to 200 C.
- Step 2: Place the tater tots in the air fryer basket for 7 to 9 minutes, shaking once midway through the cooking time.
- Step 3: Remove from the air fryer and add shredded cheddar cheese, green onions, and bacon bits.
- Step 4: Place them back in the air fryer and cook for 1 or 2 minutes until the cheese is melted.
- Step 5: Drizzle sour cream and serve.

03 CINNAMON DESSERT FRIES

- Cinnamon dessert fries offer a great way to enjoy sweet potatoes for your mid-meal snacking option that's tasty as well as healthy. This snack also serves as a great side for your lunch and dinner!
- Preparation Time: 5 minutes
- Cooking Time: 15 minutes

Servings: 4

Per serving:

Kcal: 118; Fat: 19; Carbs: 20g; Protein: 11g; Sugars: 10g; Fibre: 6g

Ingredients:

- 2 sweet potatoes
- 2 tsp. butter, melted
- 2 tsp. sugar
- ½ tsp. cinnamon

Instructions:

- Step 1: Preheat the air fryer to 180 C.
- Step 2: Peel the sweet potatoes and cut them into thin slices.
- Step 3: Coat the fries with 1 tablespoon of melted butter.
- Step 4: Cook the fries in the air fryer for 15 to 18 minutes.
- Step 5: Remove the fries from the air fryer. Place them in a bowl.
- Step 6: Coat the fries with the remaining butter. Sprinkle cinnamon and sugar. Mix gently to coat.

04 GARLIC BREAD

- Your air fryer makes it very easy for you to prepare delicious but healthy garlic bread! Best of all, you only need a few ingredients and only 10 minutes to prepare this dish.
- Preparation Time: 5 minutes
- Cooking Time: 7 minutes

Servings: 4

Per serving:

Kcal: 330; Fat: 27; Carbs: 30g; Protein: 17g; Sugars: 11g; Fibre: 9g

Ingredients:

- 8 slices of bread
- 3 tsp. butter
- 3 garlic cloves, minced
- ½ tsp. Italian seasoning
- A pinch of red pepper flakes
- 20g mozzarella cheese
- 10g grated Parmesan cheese

Instructions:

- Step 1: Preheat the air fryer to 190 C.
- Step 2: Cut the bread slices into halves.
- Step 3: Mix the butter, Italian seasoning, garlic, and red pepper flakes in a small bowl. Spread the garlic butter mixture on the top of the bread slices evenly.
- Step 4: Place the bread slices in the air fryer and cook for 6 to 7 minutes. Add the cheese when just 2 minutes are left to cook.

05 FROZEN MOZZARELLA STICKS

- This recipe offers an easy and quick way to prepare crispy mozzarella sticks without any cheese bursting out.
- Preparation Time: 6 minutes
- Cooking Time: 6 minutes

Servings: 4

Per serving:

Kcal: 540; Fat: 47; Carbs: 50g; Protein: 29g; Sugars: 19g; Fibre: 12g

Ingredients:

- 10 mozzarella sticks, frozen
- Hot sauce for dipping

Instructions:

- Step 1: Preheat the air fryer to 190 C.
- Step 2: Place the frozen mozzarella sticks in the basket of your air fryer and cook for 6 to 8 minutes.
- Step 3: Remove them from the air fryer and serve with hot sauce for dipping.

06 STUFFED MUSHROOMS

- You need just 6 ingredients and about 30 to 40 minutes to get these irresistible stuffed mushrooms ready to eat! The cheese and sausage make them filling and hearty.
- Preparation Time: 20 minutes
- Cooking Time: 15 minutes

Servings: 4

Per serving:

Kcal: 311; Fat: 27; Carbs: 29g; Protein: 16g; Sugars: 11g; Fibre: 6g

Ingredients:

- 50g Italian ground sausage
- 50g baby portabella mushroom caps
- 1 bunch spinach, chopped
- 2 tomatoes, chopped
- 25g grated parmesan cheese
- 25g of shredded mozzarella

Instructions:

- Step 1: Preheat the air fryer to 176 C.
- Step 2: Brown the Italian sausage on the stovetop over medium heat. Drain the remaining grease and set it aside.
- Step 3: Chop the tomatoes and spinach.
- Step 4: Wash the mushroom caps thoroughly and remove the stems.
- Step 5: Combine the spinach, tomatoes, sausage, and parmesan cheese. Stuff the mixture into each mushroom cap using a spoon until it is heaping full.
- Step 6: Place the stuffed mushrooms in the air fryer basket and cook for 5 minutes. Remove the mushrooms and top them with shredded mozzarella. Cook for another 3 minutes.

07 CHOCOLATE OATMEAL

- Chocolate oatmeal contains a high amount of fibre that can improve your digestion while also doubling as your post-dinner dessert.
- Preparation Time: 2 minutes
- Cooking Time: 5 minutes

Servings: 4

Per serving:

Kcal: 250; Fat: 15g; Carbs: 16g; Protein: 10g; Sugars: 8g; Fibre: 7g

Ingredients:

- 1 banana
- 50g rolled oats
- 1 tsp. maple syrup
- 1 tsp. vanilla extract
- ½ tsp. baking powder
- 1 egg
- 50ml milk
- ½ tsp. ground cinnamon
- 1 tsp. dark cocoa powder
- 10 tsp. chocolate chips

Instructions:

- Step 1: Grease the baking dish and keep them aside. Add all the ingredients except chocolate chips into a blender and blend until smooth.
- Step 2: Pour the oats batter into the prepared baking dish.
- Step 3: Place it in the air fryer and bake at 165 C for 13 to 15 minutes.

08 AVOCADO FRIES

- It is a light and crispy snack prepared with creamy avocado and breadcrumbs.
- Preparation Time: 5 minutes
- Cooking Time: 10 minutes

Servings: 4

Per serving:

Kcal: 450; Fat: 26; Carbs: 29g; Protein: 17g; Sugars: 10g; Fibre: 8g

Ingredients:

- 4 avocados
- 50g breadcrumbs
- 50g flour
- 2 eggs
- ½ tsp. garlic powder
- ½ tsp. salt
- 10 tsp. hot sauce

Instructions:

- Step 1: Preheat the air fryer to 200 C.
- Step 2: Wash the avocados and cut each into halves. Then, slice them into small wedges. Scoop out the wedges using a spoon gently keeping their shape intact.
- Step 3: Take 3 bowls. Put the breadcrumbs in the first bowl. Add the salt and garlic powder and mix to combine. Then, place the eggs and flour separately into the two other bowls. Whisk the eggs.
- Step 4: Dip each avocado wedge into the egg mixture, and then into the flour mixture. Then, dip them into the breadcrumb mixture.
- Step 5: Place the avocado wedges into the basket of the air fryer in a single layer and cook for 4 to 6 minutes, flipping halfway through. Serve with hot sauce.

09 YELLOW BANANA CHIPS

- Banan chips can be prepared in advance and stored for up to 2 months. You can eat this delicious snack anytime without worrying about too many calories added to your diet when you prepare it in your air fryer.
- Preparation Time: 5 minutes
- Cooking Time: 10 minutes

Servings: 4

Per serving:

Kcal: 140; Fat: 8g; Carbs: 12g; Protein: 6g; Sugars: 6g; Fibre: 2g

Ingredients:

- 4 large raw bananas
- ½ tsp. salt
- 1 tsp. turmeric

Instructions:

- Step 1: Preheat the air fryer to 180 C. Peel and cut raw bananas into very thin slices. Transfer them to another bowl and add enough ice water to cover them. Soak for 15 minutes and drain.
- Step 2: Place the banana slices on a towel and gently pat dry. Spritz them with cooking spray and sprinkle salt and turmeric. Toss well to combine.
- Step 3: Place the banana slices on a greased tray in an air-fryer basket in a single layer and cook for 8 to 10 minutes, stirring and turning midway through.
- Step 4: Store in an air-tight container and eat a bowlful as and when you crave a healthy and tasty snack.

10 SPICY BROCCOLI FRIES

- These soft and spicy broccoli fries are perfect to eat on cold winter days when you are looking for something to warm yourself up.
- Preparation Time: 10 minutes
- Cooking Time: 5 minutes

Servings: 4

Per serving:

Kcal: 109; Fat: 14; Carbs: 15g; Protein: 10g; Sugars: 5g; Fibre: 4g

Ingredients:

- Step 1: Preheat the air fryer to 200 C.
- Step 2: Wash the broccoli florets in water. In a bowl, add gram flour, salt, turmeric, and asafoetida. Place the broccoli florets in the gram flour mixture and toss to cover them well.
- Step 3: Lay the broccoli florets in the air fryer basket and cook for 4 to 5 minutes.

Instructions:

- Step 1: Preheat the air fryer to 200 C.
- Step 2: Wash the broccoli florets in water. In a bowl, add gram flour, salt, turmeric, and asafoetida. Place the broccoli florets in the gram flour mixture and toss to cover them well.
- Step 3: Lay the broccoli florets in the air fryer basket and cook for 4 to 5 minutes.

11   CHICKEN FRIES

- Youcan try this 10-minute chicken fries recipe in your air fryer for a quick snack! It's delicious and perfect for satisfying your taste buds craving for a spicy snack.
- Preparation Time: 5 minutes
- Cooking Time: 10minutes

Servings: 4

Per serving:

Kcal: 280; Fat: 19; Carbs: 20g; Protein: 11g; Sugars: 6g; Fibre: 3g

Ingredients:

- 100g chicken fries, frozen
- Dipping sauce of your choice

Instructions:

- Step 1: Preheat the air fryer to 180 C.
- Step 2: Thaw the chicken fries and place them on the basket of the air fryer in a single layer. Fry for 10 minutes, shaking the basket halfway through this time.
- Step 3: Serve with the dipping sauce of your choice

12   POTATO PANCAKES

- These irresistibly delicious and crispy potato pancakes get ready to eat in just 20 minutes! They are crunchy on the outside, but soft on the inside.
- Preparation Time: 10 minutes
- Cooking Time: 9 minutes

Servings: 4

Per serving:

Kcal: 344; Fat: 27; Carbs: 30g; Protein: 17g; Sugars: 12g; Fibre:10g

Ingredients:

- 30g shredded hash browns
- 3 onions
- 1 tsp. garlic, minced
- 1 tsp. of paprika
- Salt and pepper to taste
- 25g all-purpose flour
- 1 egg

Instructions:

- Step 1: Preheat your air fryer to 180 C.
- Step 2: Combine the shredded hash browns, paprika, salt, onions, garlic, pepper, flour, and egg in a bowl.
- Step 3: Prepare your pancakes. Take a 10ml measuring cup and scoop the hash brown mixture into it. Then, shake it out to get a pancake formed in the shape of the measuring cup. Then, gently press down the mixture to make it flat into the pancake form.
- Step 4: Spray the bottom of the air fryer basket generously with oil. Lay the potato cakes on the shelf of the fryer and cook for 4 to 5 minutes, and then flip. Spray the top of the pancakes with oil and cook for another 4 to 5 minutes.

13 LOADEDFRIES

- These French fries topped with bacon crumbles, melted cheddar cheese, and jalapenos offer an easy-to-prepare delicious snack that also doubles up as your go-to party food.
- Preparation Time: 10 minutes
- Cooking Time: 25minutes

Servings: 4

Per serving:

Kcal: 400; Fat: 50g; Carbs: 45g; Protein: 29g; Sugars: 13g; Fibre: 18g

Ingredients:

- 1kg potatoes
- 25g cheddar cheese
- 3 onions
- 1 tsp. onion powder
- 1 tsp. garlic powder
- ¼ tsp. basil
- ¼ tsp. paprika
- ¼ tsp. chili powder
- 20 to 25 slices of jalapeno peppers, pickled
- 4 strips of bacon, thoroughly cooked and crumbled
- Dipping sauce of your choice

Instructions:

- Step 1: Peel the potatoes and rinse them well.
- Step 2: Slice them into the shape of fries.
- Step 3: Toss the fries with the onion powder, garlic powder, and the remaining seasonings.
- Step 4: Put the fries into the air fryer basket and fry at 189 C for 20 to 25 minutes, stirring every 5 minutes.
- Step 5: Meanwhile, chop the onions.
- Step 6: Remove the fries from the air fryer and layer them on a baking sheet. Top them with bacon crumbles, cheddar cheese, jalapenos, and chopped onions.
- Step 7: Place them back in the oven and cook for another 2 minutes or until the cheese is melted.
- Step 8: Remove from oven and serve with the dipping sauce of your choice.

14 JALAPENO POPPERS

- If you want to make a delicious appetizer, you just need to throw in frozen jalapeno poppers in your air fryer and wait for the molten cheese and crispy breading to create an irresistible snack for you in just a few minutes.
- Preparation Time: 10 minutes
- Cooking Time: 10 minutes

Servings: 4

Per serving:

Kcal: 250; Fat: 25; Carbs: 26g; Protein: 15g; Sugars: 9g; Fibre: 6g

Ingredients:

- 8 jalapeno poppers

Instructions:

- Step 1: Preheat the air fryer to 180 C.
- Step 2: Place the jalapeno poppers inside the air fryer basket, leaving around 1-cm of space between them.
- Step 3: Cook for about 5 minutes and flip, cooking for another 4 minutes, or until the cheese just starts to ooze out.

15 GREEN BEAN FRIES

- Need to get your kids to eat veggies? These green bean fries cooked in your air fryer can be the perfect crowd-pleaser! Serve with their favourite sauce and enjoy a healthy and tasty snack
- Preparation Time: 10 minutes
- Cooking Time: 5 minute

Servings: 4

Per serving:

Kcal: 106; Fat: 175; Carbs: 18g; Protein: 10g; Sugars: 6g; Fibre: 3g

Ingredients:

- 500g green beans
- 1 egg
- 1 egg white
- 50g breadcrumbs
- 2 tsp. parmesan cheese, grated
- ½ tsp. garlic powder
- 1 tsp. paprika
- ¼ tsp. salt
- ⅛ tsp. ground black pepper

Instructions:

- Step 1: Preheat the air fryer to 200 C.
- Step 2: Wash and trim the green beans.
- Step 3: Whisk the egg and egg white in a bowl.
- Step 4: In another bowl, crush half of the breadcrumbs as fine as you can using the back of a spoon. These crumbs will help coat the green beans evenly. In a wide dish, combine the crushed breadcrumbs and the remaining breadcrumbs, seasoning, and parmesan cheese.
- Step 5: Place the green beans in the egg mixture, and toss to coat well, shaking off any excess egg by lifting them with a fork. Place the beans in the breadcrumb mixture and toss to cover them well.
- Step 6: Lay the breaded beans in the basket and cook for 4 to 5 minutes.

16 POTATO SKINS

- These potato skins offer a healthier alternative to your traditional pub food classic appetizers.
- Preparation Time: 15 minutes
- Cooking Time :15 minutes

Servings: 4

Per serving:

157; Fat: 19g; Carbs: 20g; Protein: 11g; Sugars: 7g; Fibre: 8g

Ingredients:

- 100g mushrooms
- 1 tsp. olive oil
- ¼ tsp. garlic powder
- 1/8 tsp. salt
- 1/8 tsp. pepper
- 3 baked potatoes
- 50g chopped ham
- 25g shredded cheddar cheese

Instructions:

- Step 1: Chop the mushrooms in halves and toss them in a bowl with garlic powder, olive oil, salt, and pepper.
- Step 2: Place the coated mushrooms in the air fryer. Cook them at 200 C for 10 minutes.
- Step 3: Remove the mushrooms from the fryer and place them in a bowl. Add chopped ham.
- Step 4: In another bowl, take the baked potatoes and cut them into halves. Scoop out the flesh gently using a spoon, leaving about 2-cm of its outer part.
- Step 5: Fill each potato skin with 1 tablespoon of cheese, and then with the mushroom and ham mixture. Place the potato skins in the air fryer and top with the remaining shredded cheddar cheese.
- Step 6: Cook the potato skins for about 5 to 8 minutes, or until the cheese melts.

17 MOZZARELLA BALLS

- These super-seasoned, bite-sized mozzarella cheese balls can be your make-ahead snack or appetizer.
- Preparation Time: 1 hour 20 minutes
- Cooking Time : 8 minute

Servings: 4

Per serving:

Kcal: 190; Fat: 25g; Carbs: 27g; Protein: 18g; Sugars: 12g; Fibre: 10g

Ingredients:

- 100g mozzarella, shredded
- 3 tsp. cornstarch
- 3 tsp. water
- 2 eggs, beaten
- 50g seasoned breadcrumbs
- 1 tsp. Italian seasoning
- 1½ tsp. garlic powder
- 1 tsp. salt
- 1½ tsp. Parmesan cheese

Instructions:

- Step 1: Add Parmesan, mozzarella, cornstarch, and water in a bowl and mix well.
- Step 2: Roll the mixture into small bite-sized balls and place them on a parchment-lined baking tray. Freeze for 40 to 50 minutes.
- Step 3: Add eggs to a bowl and whisk gently. In another bowl, stir in breadcrumbs, garlic powder, Italian seasoning, and salt.
- Step 4: Dip the cheese balls in the eggs to coat. Roll them in the breadcrumb mixture to cover them completely. Place them back on the baking sheet and put them in the freezer for about 10 minutes.
- Step 5: Remove from the freezer and dip the cheese balls in the egg mixture and roll in the breadcrumbs again.
- Step 6: Preheat the air fryer to 190 C. Place the cheese balls in the air fryer basket and cook for 8 minutes.

18   BUTTERNUT SQUASH FALAFEL

- This Butternut Squash Falafel dish is super delicious and can be a great snack when you are very hungry and looking for something filling.
- Preparation Time: 20 minutes
- Cooking Time : 60 minutes

Servings: 4

Per serving:

Kcal: 360; Fat: 28g; Carbs: 29g; Protein: 20g; Sugars: 12g; Fibre: 9g

Ingredients:

- 300g butternut squash, cubed
- 1 onion, chopped
- 1 tsp. ground cumin
- 1 clove garlic
- 1 tsp. cayenne pepper
- 1 tsp. ground coriander
- 400g chickpeas, soaked, drained, and rinsed
- 3 tbsp. fresh coriander, chopped
- 1 tsp. salt

Instructions:

- Step 1: Peel and de-seed the squash and chop it into small cubes. Mist with cooking spray and place in the air fryer. Cook for 10 to 15 minutes.
- Step 2: Once the squash is cooked, remove it from the air fryer. Add the squash to the blender along with the rest of the ingredients and blitz until the mixture feels granular.
- Step 3: Shape the mixture into 10 to 12 balls and mist them with cooking oil. Place the balls into the air fryer and cook for 10 to 15 minutes at 190 C..

19 SHISHITO PEPPERS WITH LEMON AIOLI

- Blistered Shishito Peppers are a fun snack that you can prepare in less than 10 minutes. This snack will surely be loved by all!
- Preparation Time: 5 minutes
- Cooking Time : 4 minutes

Servings: 4

Per serving:

Kcal: 270; Fat: 28g; Carbs: 30g; Protein: 19g; Sugars: 11g; Fibre: 17g

Ingredients:

- ½kg shishito peppers
- 1 tsp. avocado oil
- Lemon Aioli
- 50g vegan mayonnaise
- 1 clove garlic, finely minced
- 2 tsp. lemon juice, freshly squeezed
- 1 tsp. parsley, finely chopped
- 1 tsp. sea salt
- 1 tsp. pepper

Instructions:

- Step 1: Combine all the ingredients for the Lemon Aioli in a bowl and set aside to allow the flavours to blend.
- Step 2: Preheat the air fryer to 190 C.
- Step 3: Toss the shishito peppers with oil, and then, add them to the basket of the air fryer.
- Step 4: Fry the peppers for 4 minutes. Remove the peppers to a serving dish and sprinkle with sea salt. Serve with Lemon Aioli.

20 MAC AND CHEESE BITES

- Mac and Cheese Bites can be the perfect party snack. You can also prepare it for breakfast or as a side dish for lunch and dinner.
- **Preparation Time: 20 minutes**
- **Cooking Time : 10 minutes**

Servings: 4

Per serving:

Kcal: 150; Fat: 18g; Carbs: 20g; Protein: 9g; Sugars: 7g; Fibre: 3g

Ingredients:

- 100g cheese
- 100g macaroni
- 4 slices bacon
- 50g broccoli florets, finely chopped
- 50g cheddar cheese, shredded
- 50g French fried onions

Instructions:

- Step 1: Cook the bacon and macaroni separately in your traditional way. Top the cooked bacon with cheese and cooked macaroni, and stir in the broccoli. Mix gently to combine well.
- Step 2: Spray muffin cups with very little cooking spray. Spoon about 2 tablespoons of cheese and mac mixture into each muffin cup. Top each muffin cup with fried onions and cheddar cheese.
- Step 3: Air fry at 200 C for 6 to 8 minutes, or until the bites are golden brown. This dish goes well with tater tots and carrot fries.

21 CINNAMON SUGAR CHICKPEAS

- These cinnamon-sugar chickpeas are made with very little oil and are ready to eat in less than 30 minutes. Once cooked, you can pair the dish with cheese to create a tasty snack that satisfies you to the fullest!
- Preparation Time: 4 minutes
- Cooking Time : 17 minutes

Servings: 4

Per serving:

Kcal: 270; Fat: 29g; Carbs: 32g; Protein: 19g; Sugars: 13g; Fibre: 9g

Ingredients:

- 100g chickpeas, soaked for 8 hours and drained
- ½ tsp. cinnamon
- 1 tbsp. sugar

Instructions:

- Step 1: Preheat the air fryer to 190 C.
- Step 2: Add the drained chickpeas to the air fryer basket. Cook for 15 minutes. Shake the basket and spray the chickpeas with cooking spray and continue to fry for another 10 minutes, shaking the basket every 4 to 5 minutes for even cooking.
- Step 3: Stir together sugar and cinnamon and sprinkle half of the mixture over the chickpeas. Air fry for another 2 minutes.
- Step 4: Transfer the chickpeas to a bowl and stir in the remaining seasoning to coat well.

22 SPICY TATER TOTS

- These tater tots are so tempting that they will leave your kids asking for more. Prepared with less oil in your air fryer, you do not even have to worry about your calorie intake while gorging on these tasty bites.
- Preparation Time: 5 minutes
- Cooking Time : 25 minutes

Servings: 4

Per serving:

Kcal: 200; Fat: 18g; Carbs: 20g; Protein: 11g; Sugars: 7g; Fibre: 5g

Ingredients:

- 4 potatoes
- 1 tbsp. of avocado oil
- 2 tbsp. of all-purpose flour
- 1 tsp. of salt
- 2 tsp. of garlic powder
- 2 tsp. of onion powder
- 2 tsp. chili powder
- 2 tbsp. of ketchup

Instructions:

- Step 1: Skin the potatoes and parboil them in a pot for 7 to 10 minutes.
- Step 2: Remove the potatoes from the water and grate them with a cheese grater into a bowl.
- Step 3: Add the flour, salt, avocado oil, garlic powder, chili powder, and onion powder to the bowl. Mix well until the potatoes are evenly covered with the spice blend.
- Step 4: Rub very little avocado oil onto your hands and form the potato mixture into tater tots. Place the tater tots in the air fryer basket and air fry for 15 minutes at 190 C. Serve with ketchup.

23 CARROT FRIES

- Carrot fries give you the goodness of healthy carrots and the crispness of fries. It is a tasty and quick snack that can also be your side dish for any meal!
- Preparation Time: 5 minutes
- Cooking Time : 15 minutes

Servings: 4

Per serving:

Kcal: 120; Fat: 16g; Carbs: 18g; Protein: 12g; Sugars: 7g; Fibre: 6g

Ingredients:

- 2 carrots
- 1 tbsp. olive oil
- 2 tbsp. seasoning of your choice

Instructions:

- Step 1: Peel the carrots and slice them into "French fry" sized sticks.
- Step 2: Place the carrots in a bowl and add seasoning and oil.
- Step 3: Toss the carrots until they are well coated and place them in the air fryer basket. Air fry at 200 C for 15 minutes, shaking halfway through.

24 SEASONED PRETZELS

- Seasoned pretzels make an easy snack to prepare in your air fryer. Plus, they can also be made gluten-free.
- Preparation Time: 5 minutes
- Cooking Time : 8 minutes

Servings: 4

Per serving:

Kcal: 240; Fat: 22g; Carbs: 24g; Protein: 15g; Sugars: 10g; Fibre: 7g

Ingredients:

- 100g gluten-free pretzels
- ¼ tsp. garlic powder
- 1 tsp. onion powder
- 1 tsp. cumin powder
- 1 tsp. coriander powder
- 1 tsp. Italian seasoning
- Seasoning of your choice
- Olive oil spray

Instructions:

- Step 1: Line the basket of your air fryer with aluminium foil. Spray it with olive oil spray.
- Step 2: Place the pretzels in the air fryer basket and top them with the seasonings. Mix well so that the pretzels are evenly coated.
- Step 3: Cook in the air fryer at 190 C for 3 minutes. Remove the pretzels, and spray with olive oil spray. Place them back into the fryer and cook for another 3 minutes.

25 ROASTED EDAMAME

- This roasted edamame dish is a quick low-calorie snack. It is very easy to prepare and is ready to eat in just 15 minutes.
- Preparation Time: 5 minutes
- Cooking Time : 10 minutes

Servings: 4

Per serving:

Kcal: 102; Fat: 16g; Carbs: 17g; Protein: 10g; Sugars: 6g; Fibre: 4g

Ingredients:

- 100g Edamame
- 1 tsp. garlic salt
- Olive oil spray

Instructions:

- Step 1: Place the edamame in the air fryer basket and coat it with a dash of garlic salt and olive oil spray.
- Step 2: Air fry at 190 C for 10 minutes. Stir halfway through the cooking time. If you want the edamame to be crispier, air fry for an additional 5 minutes.

26 CORN ON THE COB

- This dish turns out sweet, crunchy, and crispy. It is ready to eat in just 15 minutes and is great to have when you are very hungry but do not want to add too many calories to your diet.
- Preparation Time: 3 minutes
- Cooking Time : 12 minutes

Servings: 4

Per serving:

Kcal: 58; Fat: 4; Carbs: 7g; Protein: 5g; Sugars: 2g; Fibre: 1g

Ingredients:

- 4 corns on the cob
- 2 tbsp. butter, melted
- 1 tsp. salt
- 1 tsp. pepper

Instructions:

- Step 1: Rinse the corn and pat dry.
- Step 2: Brush the ears of the corn with butter and then season with salt and pepper.
- Step 3: Place the corn on the shelf of the air fryer basket and air fry at 170 C for 12 minutes, turning each corn halfway through the cooking time.

27 CRISPY SEASONED BROCCOLI

- This delicious crispy broccoli can be prepared in your air fryer in just 10 minutes! It is very easy to prepare and gives you perfectly roasted and flavourful broccoli.
- **Preparation Time: 2 minutes**
- **Cooking Time : 8 minutes**

Servings: 4

Per serving:

Kcal: 170; Fat: 15g; Carbs: 18g; Protein: 11g; Sugars: 7g; Fibre: 5g

Ingredients:

- 100g broccoli florets
- ¼ tsp. garlic powder
- ¼ tsp. pepper
- ¼ tsp. salt
- 2 tsp. olive oil

Instructions:

- Step 1: Add broccoli, garlic powder, salt, pepper, and olive oil to a bowl and toss well to combine.
- Step 2: Transfer to the air fryer basket and cook at 176 C for 8 minutes, shaking halfway through.

28 RED SPICY BANANA CHIPS

- If you are looking to grab something hot and spicy, this one's just for you. These red hot and spicy banana chips will leave a lingering taste in your mouth for long enough.
- **Preparation Time: 5 minutes**
- **Cooking Time : 10 minutes**

Servings: 4

Per serving:

Kcal: 142; Fat: 9g; Carbs: 10g; Protein: 5g; Sugars: 6g; Fibre: 2g

Ingredients:

- 4 large raw bananas
- ½ tsp. salt
- 1 tsp. red chilli powder

Instructions:

- Step 1: Preheat the air fryer to 180 C. Peel and cut raw bananas into very thin slices.
- Step 2: Place the banana slices on a towel and gently pat dry. Spritz them with cooking spray and sprinkle salt and chili powder. Toss well to combine.
- Step 3: Place the banana slices on a greased tray in an air-fryer basket in a single layer and cook for 8 to 10 minutes, stirring and turning midway through.
- Step 4: Store in an air-tight container and eat whenever you crave a healthy and tasty snack.

29 OKRA FRIES

- These okra fries cooked in your air fryer can get you those crunchy and crispy bites you crave while enjoying the benefits of eating vegetables.
- **Preparation Time: 10 minutes**
- **Cooking Time : 5 minutes**

Servings: 4

Per serving:

Kcal: 108; Fat: 11; Carbs: 13g; Protein: 8g; Sugars: 4g; Fibre: 3g

Ingredients:

- 500g okra
- 50g rice flour
- ½ tsp. garlic powder
- 1 tsp. paprika
- ¼ tsp. salt
- ⅛ tsp. ground black pepper

Instructions:

- Step 1: Preheat the air fryer to 200 C.
- Step 2: Wash and trim the okra and cut them into vertical halves.
- Step 3: In a bowl, mix the rice flour and the remaining ingredients.
- Step 4: Place the okra in the flour mixture and toss to cover them, well. Lay the coated okra in the air fryer basket and cook for 4 to 5 minutes.

30 BELL PEPPER FRIES

- Bell pepper fries are a delicious and easy-to-prepare snack that works great to relieve your hunger pangs between meals!
- **Preparation Time: 5 minutes**
- **Cooking Time :15 minutes**

Servings: 4

Per serving:

Kcal: 90; Fat: 10g; Carbs: 11g; Protein: 7g; Sugars: 4g; Fibre: 2g

Ingredients:

- 5 bell peppers
- 1 tbsp. olive oil
- 2 tbsp. seasoning of your choice
- 1 tsp. salt

Instructions:

- Step 1: Cut the bell peppers into "French fry" sized sticks
- Step 2: Place the bell peppers in a bowl and add salt, seasoning, and oil.
- Step 3: Toss the bell peppers until they are well coated and place them in the air fryer basket. Air fry at 200 C for 15 minutes, shaking halfway through.

CONCLUSION

Having an air fryer can be a huge relief for those who always find it hard to choose between healthy versus tasty food. Air fryers have made it much easier for you to cook healthy dishes that also taste great.

So, now you no longer have to struggle to ensure your family eats healthy foods without making a fuss about not getting those tasty bites they crave.

Air fryers also come with many other benefits such as faster cooking time, easy cleaning, and less mess. With so many benefits, an air fryer will surely prove to be a worthy investment you have made for your health and precious time.

And in case you haven't yet purchased an air fryer for your kitchen, it's definitely the time to go ahead and welcome this new appliance.

With your air fryer, you are sure to relish your mealtimes with your family. You now have 150 tempting recipes to try in your air fryer. You can cook a combination of two or more dishes from these recipes to create a wholesome menu for your family to eat for breakfast, lunch, and dinner. Simply choose the recipes based on how hungry you feel and what you specifically feel like eating!

So, go ahead and treat your family and guests with the breakfast, dinner, lunch, vegan, and snack recipes shared with you in this book.

Happy Cooking!

REFERENCES

1. https://www.ncbi.nlm.nih.gov/pmc/articles/PMC4632424/
2. https://pubmed.ncbi.nlm.nih.gov/26457715/
3. https://www.ncbi.nlm.nih.gov/pmc/articles/PMC8825730/
4. http://epic.iarc.fr/research/acrylamide.php
5. https://www.ncbi.nlm.nih.gov/pmc/articles/PMC4164905/
6. https://www.ncbi.nlm.nih.gov/pubmed/25872656
7. https://pubmed.ncbi.nlm.nih.gov/30487558/
8. https://pubmed.ncbi.nlm.nih.gov/23731447/

Please scan the QR code below to access your bonus PDF with all 150 recipes with full coloured photos & beautiful designs alongside! This is the only way we can get the recipes with coloured photos to you & keep the book as reasonably priced as possible.

Also, once downloaded you can take the PDF with you digitally wherever you go- meaning you can cook these recipes wherever you may be! (As long as you have an air fryer!)

We hope you enjoy and do let us know your feedback!

STEP BY STEP Guide To Access-

1. Open Your Phones (Or Any Device You Want The Book On) Back Camera. The Back Camera Is The One You use as if you are taking a picture of someone.
2. Simply point your Camera at the QR code and 'tap' the QR code with your finger to focus the camera.
3. A link / pop up will appear. Simply tap that (and make sure you have internet connection) and the
4. FREE PDF containing all of the coloured images should appear.
5. Now you have access to these FOREVER. Simply 'Bookmark' The tab it opened on, or download the document and take wherever you want.
6. Repeat this on any device you want it on! (If you want it on a laptop, simply email the document to yourself!)
7. Any issues please email us at *vicandersonpublishing@gmail.com* and we will be happy to help!!

Printed in Great Britain
by Amazon

17868110R00102